Food and Forgiveness:
How a Chicago Chef
Came Around

Food and Forgiveness:
How a Chicago Chef
Came Around

GREG CHRISTIAN

FOOD AND FORGIVENESS:
HOW A CHICAGO CHEF
CAME AROUND

Copyright © 2009
by Greg Christian

cover design by Lucy Swerdfeger

Published by

White Eagle Press
Chicago, Illinois

ISBN:
978-0-9824706-0-2 — $ 19.95*

*Ten percent of the royalties from this book
are donated to the ORGANIC SCHOOL PROJECT.

www.gregchristianconsulting.com

Printed in the United States of America

To my parents
~Norm and Kathryn~
without whom I would not be here,
were it not for the miracle of life.

Sweet are the uses of adversity,
Which, like the toad, ugly and venomous,
Wears yet a precious jewel in his head;
And this our life, exempt from public haunt,
Finds tongues in trees, books in the running brooks,
Sermons in stones, and good in every thing.

As You Like It, Act 2, scene 1, 12–17

Table of Contents

Chapter One
Emergency!

"LISTEN TO ME! Your daughter could die!"

For the third time, I reeled back in panic and uncertainty as the ER staff followed the doctor's lead and glared at me with contempt.

Yes, I had been drinking. Only a few short minutes before I had been at home chugging Heineken and shouting with my buddies as we watched a Bears' game.

"Don't you even know the medications your daughter takes?" demanded the brittle doctor as she continued to berate me. Of course I didn't know. That was my wife's job. Edita took care of all that stuff. My job was to bring home the money, thank you very much.

"I'm not sure," was all I could say in response to the attack. "I know she's allergic to milk and nuts and peanuts."

"I need to know *everything* she's allergic to!"

"Doctor, my wife isn't answering her portable phone," I replied.

"I can't talk to you anymore," she jeered as she stormed away. She had a short hair cut, was about five feet five inches tall, and must have been in her early fifties. And she held her left hand in her pocket, strutting around like a puffed up little Napoleon.

Britha, my daughter, was scarcely six years old, and her unchecked asthma was threatening to incite a heart attack. At least I knew that much. If that damned nebulizer at home had worked, I wouldn't even be here at the hospital.

For the first three years of her life, Britha was symptom free of allergies. Then the asthma attacks began to manifest, and we found ourselves consulting allergist after allergist, looking for answers and cures. And we were slow to realize the magnitude of the problem. A visitor's perfume might cause a delayed outburst of Britha's asthma, or the stray cat fur left on the sofa from a friend's jacket might do the same.

Identifying the triggers for a person's asthma attacks is essential, and with Britha it seemed as if almost everything in her environment was a trigger. Besides perfumes and animal fur, at least eighty percent of her food created conditions that brought out her asthmatic response. Dust was another large contributor, and when we realized how extensive a problem it was, we went and got plastic for all of the mattresses and pillows. We also put duct-tape on the zippers of all of our pillows.

My wife Edita's family was Filipino, so our two daughters were always watched by extended family. At first we trusted both of our families to prepare food for Britha, and we would check out their intended menu ahead of time. Yet despite our best efforts, it always seemed that something additional was added, or that they forgot to tell us about one of the items that they planned to include, and Britha would come down with an attack. Finally, in frustration, we would prepare Britha's food before we took her for sitting, but then, God bless him, my wife's father, Rafael, would sneak a treat to Britha that she was not supposed to have. We would ask my mother not to wear perfume, but she still did. People just didn't get it, how serious Britha's asthma was.

One time, my wife's sister and sister-in-law, both nurses, agreed to watch Britha, and although we reviewed everything with them and they said they understood, they ended up giving her potato chips, totally setting the kid off. Go figure. All these people, especially our family, were totally out to lunch!

We also lugged our nebulizer, a gift from Carl Berman, a dear friend who gave me my start in the catering business. Carl owned a medical supply business and generously gave us a nebulizer to assist Britha in her breathing and to ward off any imminent attacks, because we didn't have health insurance since I was self-employed. The device was ten inches by ten inches by eight inches, and we bought the recommended medicines to go with it. The first two would attempt to dissipate an attack, and the third was a steroid to prevent the need to go to the hospital. Yet people had trouble learning how to use the nebulizer, and it became more trouble than it was worth, so rather than rely on it, we opted instead never to leave her out of our sight. What remained frightening was that the attacks could manifest immediately or happen a couple of hours later. A quick trigger might be from a tuft of cat fur or a peanut, whereas dust could bring delayed reactions. There was a lot of cleaning of clothes and sheets, not to mention of Britha herself.

As I stood in the emergency room, watching my youngest daughter gasping for air and the attendants doing their best to help her, one of Britha's earlier and scariest episodes came flooding over my consciousness. It was the time when Edita and I almost lost her, during a family trip to Toronto.

We went up to Canada a lot, because my wife had a lot of family there, and one time we decided to go by train, which takes about twelve hours. By then we had graduated to a handheld, battery-operated nebulizer, and Edita always had everything organized and ready for Britha, like the wipes to clean the hands and stuff like that. Along with some of the things I had packed for us for lunch were some cookies from Albert's café that did a lot of my wholesale baking. We had finished our salmon but, as soon as Britha had eaten one of the cookies, she went right into vapor lock, her trachea constricting as she labored to breathe. I didn't realize it then, but there were ground pecans in the cookie dough, and that's what caused her reaction.

There was no help to be found on the train and stopping the train was out of the question. All my wife could do was to hold Britha tightly to her, mustering all the love and prayers that she could to rescue our daughter, in the way that a mother and daughter can become almost one being. And during those crucial twenty minutes, it must have been only through the grace of God that Edita was able to save Britha.

"Mr. Christian," announced one of emergency room nurses, shaking me from my memory. "We do not have the necessary resources here to help your daughter. A special trauma team has been dispatched from the university hospital at Loyola, and they will be here in a few minutes."

The team arrived shortly thereafter and, without even speaking to the attending physician, they took Britha's charts and secured her in their transport, relaying all of the information and their observations to the doctors at university hospital. Before I knew it, they were wheeling Britha out the door, having told me that I would have to follow them, that I couldn't ride in their ambulance.

I went over to Britha and told her that she would be going for a short ride and that I would be following her. Racing after them in my little, Chicago-style, white Mitsubishi Mirage, a flood of images and worries cascaded across my mind. I felt like a heel for what had happened and completely helpless. I also knew that I had broken my promise to Edita. The endless bullshit loop raced through my mind — 'Your daughter might die.' 'I'm in deep, serious trouble.' 'Your daughter could have a heart attack. We can't help her.' 'I told my wife I wasn't gonna have the guys over for the game, but I did it anyway.'

When I arrived at university hospital, they were hitting Britha hard with IVs and she was already hooked up to all kinds of monitors. They said that they had no place for Britha in their intensive care ward, but less than ten minutes later, they announced that a place had been found and that the doctor from that ward was on her way down to interview me. It was obvious that they had done this before, and that they knew what they were doing. Their confidence in what they were doing gave me a sudden burst of hope that Britha would be fine.

As I waited for the new doctor, I noticed how different the hospital itself was. It was a happier hospital. It had a totally different look from the first place, with none of the drab institutional colors, but instead bright yellows and reds that were more vibrant and alive. The first place had felt like a geriatric ward, whereas this place was happy and young.

The new doctor was wonderful. She explained that Britha would be fine, and that it wasn't as bad as the first physician had suggested. She was calm and cool and sat on a desk and let me sit in her chair as she asked questions, some of the answers to which she wrote on her hand and arm. Her whole composure was much softer and more reassuring.

It felt like I was with a kindergarten teacher, one full of love. She was so cool! She never left me alone and let me follow her and be with Britha. I felt embraced and affirmed by her genuine compassion and reassurance, and I'll never forget her.

By the time we got settled into the intensive care unit, it was quiet and dark. It was only Britha and me, and when she would look at me with her penetrating brown eyes, I could only feel a silent, endless loop of desperation swirling within me crying, 'I can't help you. I'm really sorry. I can't help you.'

Because she had lost her mother and three siblings in a tragic car accident, Edita avoided hospitals like the plague. We all have some aversion like that, and Edita's was hospitals. So I was the one who stayed with Britha those next five days, fully feeling her fear and watching her wide-eyed wonder at all that was happening, when she wasn't sleeping from all of the drugs that they were giving to her.

We kept searching for allergists who could help, as we struggled to figure out what was triggering Britha's attacks. We learned that reactions that manifested from these so-called triggers and that some, like cat dander or peanuts, would bring an immediate, full-blown attack, while others, like dust, would bring a less severe attack maybe a couple of hours after exposure. It was like trying to add one plus one, but not knowing what the specific variables were. You really feel blind and helpless. It turned out that eighty percent of the triggers were related to food, with almost everything else to cologne or dust, although cat dander was a major trigger. And as much as we did, it never seemed to be quite enough.

We sought allergist after allergist, hoping to find there was someone who could help Britha so that she could enjoy a normal life. We finally met with a leading expert, a professor of medicine, who practiced in Oak Park. Britha was about seven and as she and Edita and I waited in the sitting room, my mother barged in unannounced, having driven all the way from Wisconsin. We had told her about our consultation, but we never imagined that she would come. When we could see the doctor, we all went in, and she talked with us for about half an hour and reviewed Britha's voluminous records. Finally, she announced, "I want you to give Britha steroids every day for the next five years and she'll be fine."

At hearing this, it felt like I had been punched in the gut. Britha had a very adverse reaction to steroids. They made her feel as if she wanted to crawl out of her own skin. She would relentlessly bang her head on the floor. They literally transformed her into a little stoned zombie, and I could always see her eyes go dull just before she switched into something that was definitely not our daughter. Whenever we had given her steroids before and she had manifested this reaction, I would just cry and apologize to her that we had to do it. It was a horrible sight, and I couldn't even imagine what a daily, five year regimen of it would do to her, both physically and emotionally. My mother was a basket case, weeping and mustering all of her power to elicit from the doctor a promise that her prescribed treatment would guarantee that Britha would not die. And Edita was already freaked out; taking care of Britha had become her full-time job.

When we left the doctor's office, we said goodbye to my mom and thanked her for coming. As Britha, Edita and I walked back to our car, Edita turned to me and said, "We are going to go *all* alternative medicine and *all* organic food."

I said, "Okay. You're the boss."

We walked on a bit, and I added, "I'm not sure about the organic food idea. After all, I know food."

I didn't press further, but wanted to, big ego and all, because I knew we were under total duress and worried sick for not only Britha's health but for her survival. It had been a shocking meeting, our future uncertain and a major turning point had been reached.

As we embarked upon this new path, Edita began to research alternative medicine, looking for contact information and references for various homeopaths, acupuncturists, chiropractors and energy healers. I fought against the organic food plan, indicating that we just couldn't afford it. Edita's determined response was, "You'll just have to figure that out, because this is what we are going to do."

We first found a wonderful homeopath from India who was also a medical doctor. She helped us enormously that first year, and we found that whatever we were doing, including eating only organic food, was working and that we were no longer in the hospital emergency room with Britha every two or three weeks. However, the required regimen of pills and jars became untenable after a year, and Edita found a chiropractor who also used kinesiology and energy work to take us to the next level of healing. He started clearing Britha of her food allergies and somehow he knew the correct order in which to do so and he also put her on a special diet. All of his work proved beneficial, but his office was an hour and a half away, and after a year of such a long drive, Edita searched for a new healer who lived closer to our home.

We next found Dr. Moniligod, a venerable Filipino western medical doctor who was also an expert in the practice of the Japanese healing technique called Mahikara that uses divine light to clear inner blocks. Dr. Moniligod also used kinesiology, but curiously would start with things that had nothing to do with what Britha ate. Nevertheless, she successfully cleared Britha of every remaining allergy except peanuts. Today Britha can babysit a cat with no problem!

I would often take Britha to her appointments with Dr. Moniligod. More often than not, I would fall asleep, hung over, in the waiting room. The good doctor soon asked if I would like a treatment, too, and I thought, "Why not?" So she started giving me treatments of the divine light that she had learned how to share. Now I am not allergic to anything, except beer and vodka. But I loved the treatments and deeply believe that those six months of treatments from Dr. Moniligod played a very real and beneficial role in how my life, with all of its contradictions, trials and tribulations, would later evolve.

It wasn't long before Edita would join Britha and me in our forays into the field of alternative medicine and the many helpful treatments that it can afford its patients. It took Britha about two and a half years to get better. Today she is a member of her high school's field hockey team, a team that recently won a state championship. Of course, during that entire interval, I remained blinded by my own preconceptions of what food was as well as by my rigorous culinary training to discover any useful insights. Reflecting back on those years, I now realize that I deliberately discounted any potential benefit and role that our family's eating organic food may have played in Britha's return to full health. Those connections would come later, after a great deal of self-searching, introspection and emotional pain. I doubt if I was ready for them at that time. To have understood all that had helped Britha become whole would have required my looking in that same way at myself and acknowledging the many lacks, wants, and doubts.

It is my experience that if we are committed to knowing and loving truth, wherever it takes us, we need to be prepared for some unexpected and surprising journeys. My own journeys would take me to the far corners of the earth and as well as to some of the deepest crevices within myself.

I will remain forever grateful to Edita for her steadfast refusal to leave any stone unturned or any avenue of healing unexplored until we found what successfully restored Britha to full health. I would have helped, but didn't know how, and Edita was better suited to that challenge. I know, though, that a very deep part of me has always wanted to help others who were in need — even as early as when I was three years old.

Chapter Two
A Desire to Help

MY EARLIEST RECOLLECTION is that of my mother weeping during the aftermath of the assassination of President John F. Kennedy. Such epic moments, be it from the death of a president on November 22, 1963 or from the deaths of thousands of New Yorkers on September 11, 2001, leave indelible imprints on both the psyche and the heart.

As my mother lay on our living room sofa watching the television reports and weeping, my heart burned to comfort her, for I could see her grief and feel her desolation. But all I could do was to sit there in silence, yearning to help, but not knowing how. God knows she had her hands full, raising six of us kids while my dad, a very successful drummer in a rock band, was on the road giving concerts with his band. Sometimes he was even gone for a couple of months. Both of my parents worked very hard.

Ten days prior to the Kennedy assassination, I had just celebrated my third birthday. Now, looking back, I have come to understand that my mother's profound grief at that time instilled very deeply into my temperament and personality a life-long desire to help, to serve others. And since I was the oldest of my siblings, Connie was born in 1962 and Nancy in 1963, with Jeff due to come in 1964, to be followed later by Julie and Norman. That gave me more than ample an opportunity to extend help to my mom, since my dad was away so much with his band. I always wanted to help. When I was only four, I remember helping some men paint our family's garage, and them laughing at me, because I didn't want to take my shirt off. They all had their shirts off, and I didn't want them to see my scrawny little chest. But they insisted, and that was my first major upset.

One of the strangest things that ever happened to me took place when I was between the ages of three and five, and it was something that I came to understand much later in life. I awoke from a dream one night and was terrified to see all kinds of exotic animals' heads on the walls and ceiling of my bedroom, as well as on the walls of the bathroom and hallways. They were vividly alive and in full color, and their heads were constantly moving. I raced into my parents' bedroom and woke them up to tell them what I had seen; however, they calmly told me that it was a dream and that I should go back to bed. Their casual attitude allayed my initial fear and concern, and I began to feel safe. But it wasn't a dream. I could see the animals with my eyes wide open, even though nobody else saw them.

These animals' heads would appear frequently at night for the next couple of years. Some were easily recognized, like the hippopotamus and tiger, from their pictures in zoo books, but others I had never seen before. They weren't angry, ever, and there were hundreds of them. As I became familiar with them, they were in fact my subtle companions. Much later in life, I would learn that children between the ages of three and six are predominantly in theta most of the time, and that theta induces an altered state of consciousness that can open doors to other domains and dimensions. I now wonder if these so-called imaginary friends of children of this age are perhaps not that imaginary after all. Some day we may evolve enough as a species to know more about the invisible worlds that apparently surround us.

In 1965 I entered the first grade at St. Peter The Apostle School in Itasca. Diligent and quiet as a student, and wanting to learn as much as I could, and I rarely got in trouble. The only incident that I remember from that first year was during lunch, when we stood up for grace before the meal. I stood up, clicked my heels together, and gave a Nazi salute. I must have observed it in a war movie. I didn't even know what it all meant. But, as fortune would have it, the nun who was our principal was looking right at me when I did it, and I was given a severe dressing down shortly thereafter. Most of my memories of those five years at Emory Day are of playing at recess, even though we had to go to church very early every morning. Our playground was the church parking lot, and we played tag and baseball and had races. At the back of the parking lot were a lot of trees that bore fruit that we called horse apples, and we would pick up the ones that had fallen and throw them at each other. Once a month, or so, we had 'hot dog day' and one time my dad was able to volunteer and come as a chaperone, and I thought that was way cool.

In fourth grade, I had a crush on Christy Reda, and all of the girls picked her up and the guys picked me up and made us kiss. It was really embarrassing. I also began to question some of the things that we were being taught, because it didn't feel 'true' to me, although I could tell that my teachers believed whatever it was they were telling us, so I always had questions, which didn't endear me to my teachers.

We lived about three miles from the school, and the daily bus trips were a blast, mostly because there was all kinds of action on the bus. What better way to start your day than riding in a bus full of wild kids? One day, though, there was a blizzard and the buses couldn't pick us up, and we had to walk all those miles to school. That was even better.

When I was seven years old, and in second grade, I had my First Communion at St. Peter's, and I was terrified, because there was so much to remember for the ceremony and such enormous pressure to do everything perfectly. Would I remember my vows? Would the host drop out of my mouth? Since I was almost always the shortest kid in class, I had the unenviable position of going first. However, after I got through all of that, the party that followed at home was truly where it was at! There must have been two hundred people, all dressed up.

That same year was the year Chicago received a huge amount of snow. Two things particularly stand out for me about that sudden onslaught of white: the first was how I saved my sister Nancy's life, and the second was how I finally learned how to lose myself, to disappear, in some sort of repetitive task. The beginnings of my ability to disappear had manifested several years earlier, when I was around four and five years old and my mom's mom, who was Bohemian and Irish, allowed me to help with the dishes, something that my mom would never let me do. Recognizing a special driven quality in my nature and will, together with my desire and willingness to help, my grandmother would set up a milk crate or chair and I would go at her dishes for hours until they made me go to bed. I didn't know what I was doing. In fact, I'm sure I was washing the same dishes over and over, but there was something mesmerizing about the hand movements that just took me to a different place. My hand would almost heat up as I abandoned myself to the various motions that I would endlessly repeat. And there was something about getting up to a certain speed that felt really good, and then I would just disappear, only coming out of it if I was interrupted or if it was time to go to bed.

But first, Nancy. She was only five that winter and all of the snowbanks stood well over her head. There was so much snow that we were sometimes literally walking on crusts that were as high as four or five feet above ground level. The house next door had a driveway that would ease down into its basement, although anyone driving by would think that it was level, owing to the snow and how it had drifted. Nancy and I were walking along in that direction, and she slipped into a concealed crevice. When I looked down into it, it was really deep, and I knew that I had to dig her out, rather than run for help. I didn't panic. I just knew what I had to do and I did it. Most people think there is only a fight or flight response, and that they have to do one or

13

the other. But there is a third option called 'standing strong' that the Blackfoot Native Americans talk about. However, only a handful of people have this ability. It means that one appears to freeze, but is instead assessing a situation and ready to take charge of it. I must have looked like a dog digging a hole as I went to work for what seemed an eternity; finally, I was able to reach her and to pull her up. When we went home and told mom, she nearly had a coronary.

During that big snow of '68, I literally shoveled from morning until dusk for five days, except when my mother made me come in to eat. It was nothing for me to do that. I never even got tired. When I was a little older I found a similar venue for escape when I was rolling, banding, and bagging the papers for my paper route. I had two *Tribune* routes, which I serviced on foot. It was easy to throw myself into the task, and I loved seeing how fast I could go.

At sixteen, after a couple years of caddying, which I didn't like, I got a job at Dominick's grocery store, and early on I challenged Jerry, the adult bagger, who was the fastest bagger, to a friendly contest. I would have some awareness of where I was, but I would get into this other place where my brain wouldn't work, and everything would just happen automatically. On Saturdays we would have fun seeing who could bag the fastest. It was never about competition, but rather about doing a good job.

The real fun at Dominick's came with sorting the soda bottles that were returned for a deposit. They came in eight packs. They would let me go back and sort them every so often, and I was able to convince my boss to save all of the bottles for me from Saturdays, and I would go in on Sundays and become a whirling dervish and disappear. The bottle pile was ten feet high. It would have been a nightmare to most kids, but all I could say was, "Let me at it!"

Whether we call it the "zone" or something else, the key to "flow" is to first tune one's self to something very repetitive and trying to go faster and faster. At least that's what worked for me. Later I developed rituals for turning this ability on, and I went from clunky to not so clunky. After a while, you can just make it happen. After about six months, I graduated to help in the produce department and I realized that I could have some autonomy, be left alone. At least initially, that was important to turning flow on and off. I was seventeen, and they would come and take pictures of my produce rack and potato rack. For me, it was all about getting it done with efficiency and speed, and all of this was perfect preparation for my eventual training as a chef and working in concert with others.

What I would later do in the kitchen, because of this gift, was to create a few rituals to turn the ability on. I would go get a cutting board and wet towel, which was used to hold the board in place, after making sure that my space was clean. I would, on purpose, waste motion, because I wanted to quiet myself in the atmosphere of the kitchen and all that was happening. All I have ever needed to get into "flow" has been to get my knife and put a pan on the fire and get the salt and pepper and place it in front of my cutting board, and I'm there, wherever 'there' is. In centering myself in preparation for entering flow, I still prefer to be alone, at least for a few minutes. My experience has been exactly that as portrayed by Kevin Costner in the film *For the Love of the Game*.

Whenever I get into flow, thinking stops and everything happens automatically, and I end up cooking with other senses, rather than the obvious ones like sight and taste. It's like stepping into another world from the world you're already in. On a few occasions, I've cooked with other chefs who can do this same thing, and when we all had finished our preparations, no one was quite sure which he had made. And when you're in flow, you automatically intuit what others need. There are some expert chefs whose talents are incredible, better than I could ever manage, but who cannot enter into flow. I believe those chefs who can enter into flow can, through the food they create, deeply touch their customer's souls. I don't know if one is born with this or if one can learn it; it can probably be both. I'm just grateful that I've got this ability and that I can use it to serve those for whom I cook.

Looking back now, I realize that it was my dad who inspired my interest in the culinary arts. Whenever he was home on weekends, he would make a special meal on Sunday and he would always experiment. It wasn't always dinner; it could be breakfast or lunch, too. I'll never forget his infamous red wine soup that got us kids a bit merry after which he incurred the immediate wrath of my mom. She was from Irish-Bohemian descent, and my dad's family was Italian. She forbade any of us kids to learn how to play musical instruments; apparently one itinerant musician in the house was more than enough.

My dad always thought outside the box, and his culinary creations never lacked imagination and the zest of experimentation. He would sometimes make a really fine, soft polenta dish, with chicken, herbs and cheese, all topped off with a tomato sauce that has really good chunky tomatoes. Other times he would serve smoked fish and caviar, filling our table with all kinds of possible spreads and sauces that we would then plop on our toast. We ate lots of pasta that dad would make, wild pastas like cauliflower. He would cut up the most minuscule pieces you could imagine, but it almost always tasted great.

Occasionally, dad would get some outlandish idea in his head, and that would dictate his future course. I remember when he believed that the thinner you cut the garlic clove, the more flavor it would give to the sandwich. He would use a razor blade, to get paper thin cuttings, that he then made it into a delectable raw garlic sandwich with Italian bread

16

from D'Amato's bakery, the last place in Illinois that uses a coal-burning oven to bake its bread. However, my mom hated raw garlic sandwiches and I think she saw them as a form of child abuse.

When I was about twelve, my dad and I got really sick, but not from garlic sandwiches. We had the runs and were vomiting for a day and half. It finally began to clear in the middle of the night, and since we were both starving by that time, we went down to the kitchen to eat something. My dad said, "Let's start with a garlic sandwich." At that time we were living in a mansion that my dad's dad owned. When my mom heard the commotion in the kitchen, she quickly came downstairs and walked in, only to observe us chomping down garlic sandwiches. She *so* lost it!

My dad's flare for making exotic meals spurred my desire to learn how to cook. And I found that I really loved to cook. Wanting to be helpful to my mom, I started with breakfast, and loved learning how to make a perfect egg. Pancakes and waffles soon followed. I would buy my mom presents, like a broom or a waffle iron, and she would just bawl. And then I would say, "Don't cry. I'll make the waffles. I'll use the broom." Raising six kids, with no car to escape, couldn't have been easy. It got to a point where I would make pancakes, waffles, eggs, and bacon every Saturday, and I loved experimenting with different batters. And everyone appreciated my efforts, too. My dad's Italian mom really showed my mom how to cook. Her family tended toward beef stews and casseroles, bland as bland could be. My mom's speciality, however, was a kind of manicotti, a homemade crepe. She cooked that when she had time, but it was mostly sandwiches for lunch every day and rarely a hot breakfast — instead, we had oatmeal, cereal, and fresh fruits. And we always had vegetables.

My love for and fascination about food also grew from the enormous and wonderful holiday meals my Italian grandmother would make. We lived a block and a half away from her house, and we weren't allowed in the kitchen during those large family parties, but I gradually figured out how to get in. My grandfather was a composer/musician and the time he could spend with us grand kids each week was a couple of hours at most. On Christmas, however, he would put down his pen and come in for dinner, which lasted a long time. I loved him, and I was one of his favorite grandchildren. He drove a big, black Imperial, because of their huge trunks that could accommodate a full set of drums. He would also take me to church sometimes when it was empty and we would just sit there together in silence.

At holiday times, my dad and I would go visit my grandfather, and he would take us around the kitchen to sample what was being prepared. Later on, I arranged to get into the kitchen by taking my grandfather a present, something edible that he would like, such as salami, imported provolone, olives, and D'Amato's bread and Bari's giardinera. I would be admitted to see him, and then we would make our sampling walk around the kitchen. The holiday meals were huge and fabulous and prepared in two separate kitchens, and usually only the women were allowed to be present in those rooms during meal preparation.

My grandfather always looked out for me. When I was ten, I was hit by a car, and I found out much later that he had made contact with the hospital staff and taken gifts to assure that I would receive the very best of care.

We had moved to Oak Park, into that kind of neighborhood full of trees and large houses. It was dusk, a school night, and I was returning home from the library and was almost home. A lady drove up to the crosswalk and didn't see me, and stepped on the gas when I was right in front of her. Even though she didn't see me, she heard me scream and she stopped the car on my right foot, having just run over my left knee. She jump out and walked to the back of her big car and then to the front, and when she saw me, she just about crapped in her pants. I'm sure she still has nightmares about it. She stood there in her sunglasses with a cigarette in her hand.

After I screamed, I was totally calm. This warmth came over me, and I watched her as she approached the front of the car. I said to her calmly, "Lady, back the car up. You're on my foot."

She freaked out and jumped back into her car and backed it up so that the car was off my foot. By this time I was surrounded by other adults. My mom was in the bathroom putting her makeup on and heard my scream and she came running out in her bathrobe. My Aunt Silvia got the call from one of my cousins, and she literally ran several blocks to see what she could do to help. The ambulance came and took me to the hospital. Shortly after I got there, my dad and Uncle Brian showed up. About an hour later, they took me to have X-rays, and they were astonished to find that nothing was broken. They couldn't believe it, because of the size of the car that had run over me and my size. I was always on the small side. So the doctors X-rayed me again and called it a miracle. I now consider it the second miracle of my life, after that of being born. I even went to school the next day.

However, my knee wouldn't stop bleeding, and after three or four days I went to a different doctor, who said that I should never have left the hospital until my left knee had healed. I needed skin grafts, and had to go into the hospital for ten or twelve days. I was fortunate to get Dr. Curtain, who was just on the verge of retirement, and was one of the city's most famous skin graft experts. I also had a second cousin who was a medical doctor, and he made sure that I had the best of care. And my grandfather came to pay off the nurses to ensure that I was getting the very best of everything, and I began to think 'This hospital stuff isn't so bad.' One of my fondest memories was of when one of my aunts showed up with a six pack of Dr. Pepper, because we weren't allowed to drink soda, but since I had almost lost my leg, my dad let it slide.

The worst of it was the frequent change of bandages, and I asked everyone to leave the room because the pain was so great. But I let my cousin Harold stay, and he would hold my hand. Harold was the smartest guy I knew. He would let me ask questions of him all night, whereas after five minutes most people would tell me that I couldn't ask any more questions. But Harold never stopped me and we would talk all night. He would also take me out for pizza and sometimes to the old Chicago stadium to see the Hawks' games. Harold was a genius and was born with a silver spoon in his mouth. He never had to work, and was always in school. He was a concert pianist and had gone to law school as well as to medical school. But he also had some really serious shortcomings that ultimately made his life very tragic, and he died alone in a wheelchair in Florida some years later. He left each of us kids twelve hundred bucks.

My hospital visit wasn't as bad as the time that I was bitten by the dog the year before. That easily has to be the most embarrassing day of my life. A dog started chasing me one day when I was going home, growling and growling and finally biting me right in the ass, and all I could do was to keep running for home. When I burst in the front door, I saw that my mom was hosting a Tupperware party and all of her friends were there, smoking their Virginia Slims and drinking their Manhattans. They all just stopped and asked, "What's wrong?"

I said, "Nothing."

And then my mother replied, "You just burst in here screaming and crying, so what's wrong?"

The next thing I knew was that I had fifteen women standing there looking at my bare ass, where I had been bitten. I just lay there, humiliated. A lot of people get bitten by dogs, and it's more frightening than dangerous. I think I had to go get a tetanus shot.

Before my parents got divorced, we all lived in Woodale, and it was great. We lived in a community that was near a lot of abandoned farm land. My fondest memories are of the endless hours of exploration, play and laughing that I shared with my siblings and friends. That unrestricted freedom certainly afforded us adventures that only children can experience, before they become burdened with adult obligations and responsibilities. I suspect that my mom saw our outdoor meanderings as her one door to freedom.

Jeff and I shared a room in the basement. He was a natural climber and the wildest of all of us kids, and he preferred the top bunk, so he got it. We'd often talk late into the night. The kitchen led off to a large backyard and patio, and during summers we would eat outside on the picnic table.

It's hard enough to raise two children, much less six. And since my dad was away a majority of the time, as I grew older, I was given more and more responsibility, especially the care of my younger brothers and sisters. As I helped them make their way in the world, I also realized that I would need to make provision for making my own way. When I was about twelve, I remember my dad sitting down with me to talk about college and saying, "Kid, you're on your own." It was not in an unloving way; rather, it was merely direct and honest. I knew that I would have to start looking out for myself, as well as for my college finances, so I watched for opportunities to make and save money and was able, a couple of years later, to get two *Tribune* paper routes, each for seven days a week. Most kids I knew growing up were afraid of their parents, who were always whacking them. I could hardly believe my friends when they would ask, "Aren't you afraid of your father?" Afraid of my dad, never! He *never* raised his voice; he was my best friend.

When I was thirteen, I remember coming home from school and telling my mom that I didn't want to go to church any more. And she said, "Okay." She is a remarkable and resilient woman. I had become increasingly uncomfortable with some of the assertions that I was hearing at school, because I didn't believe what I was being told. I didn't believe it and I didn't buy it. I also felt uncomfortable when I went on a tour of the church that was given to us prospective choir boys. The whole atmosphere was foreboding and dark, and I decided then and there that I wanted no part of it.

When I got to high school, I was enrolled mostly in honors courses, but I knew that I would still have to figure out a way to pay for college. A friend of mine, Mark Tegge, told me about the Evans scholarship, where if you caddied for a couple of years and were good in school, and also needed the financial support, they would pay for your college education, provided you made the cut after the interviews. So I started caddying at fourteen, with the sole goal of receiving an Evans scholarship. In truth, I didn't like caddying; the caddy master was one of the meanest men I had ever met and a lot of the other caddies were older men who were gamblers and drunks. Nevertheless, I was good at it and I stuck it out for two summers, even though I hated it, just so I could apply for an Evans scholarship. When I turned sixteen, I quit caddying, and applied to work at Dominick's. And poor Mark. He didn't get a scholarship, but I did, and he was really mad.

Later, when I was fifteen, my mother decided to get a divorce, and we suddenly found ourselves homeless. Years later I asked my dad what had happened. He said that no matter how much money he made on the road with his band, it never seemed to be enough to satisfy my mother. One year he made over $ 100,000, but he knew that he was killing himself, and he didn't feel that he could keep that pace up and keep his health at the same time.

After their divorce, my father's mom wouldn't let us live in my grandpa's house any longer. My brother Jeff, who was eleven, and I were sent to live with our Aunt Lil and her son Harold for two months. Aunt Lil was really old and she would give us money to go out and eat. Jeff and I had a ball discovering a whole new freedom in exploring and looking for the very best food we could find. She would also take us all out to a really fancy dinner, at least twice a year.

My uncle bought a house for my mom and us kids, but my mom had to work all the time. We had crock pot dinners five times a week. I sort of became the instant dad, and did a lot of work around the house, getting my younger siblings' lunches ready for school. When I helped in the house, I liked making dinner and the salads. But outside, I did most of the work that needed to be done. I enjoyed all of it, because I wanted to help. And for the next two summers, I caddied. At sixteen I discovered girls and quit the Oak Park High School Chess Club. My work as a bagger at Dominick's, and later in its produce department, allowed me to begin saving money for college. In 1978, when I was still seventeen, I graduated from Oak Park High School.

Chapter Three
Culinary School and First Jobs

TOWARD THE END OF HIGH SCHOOL, I was named an Evans Scholar, owing to my caddying days, and accepted its full scholarship for pre-med studies at Northwestern University. Throughout my entire childhood, my grandfather had always told me that I was going to become a doctor, so much so, that I had finally believed him. Looking back on his words today, I realize that he was actually saying to me, "Greggo, my boy, you are a healer." Wouldn't life be a lot smoother if we could discern the truth of such insights *before* we had to learn about ourselves the hard way?

While a student at Northwestern, I lived in a fraternity house for Evans Scholars. I remember looking up at the dark ceiling of my room the night before the first day of classes, saying to myself over and over again, 'I *don't* want to be a doctor.' I lay there, thinking of all the difficult courses I had taken to qualify for pre-med studies: math, science, organic chemistry. The realization was nothing less than an epiphany, and all I could do was lie there and exclaim, 'Oh, my.' Finally, I got out of bed and started to walk the halls of the Evans Scholars' House. I was drawn to some music that was playing at some remote place in the building, music that I had never heard before, but I couldn't find where it was coming from. It was very late at night and, almost as if I were in a dream, I suddenly found myself in the last room in the last hallway, where I was newly anointed in emanating blue light and the strains of The Grateful Dead.

Suddenly, I no longer had any sense of direction for my life, and chilling out with these dudes was all I wanted to do. In fact, over the next couple of years, I would attend forty concerts by the Dead. I had no interest in going to class, and would simply skip class and cram for finals. I found that if I couldn't get the stuff I had crammed into my head out in the first forty-five minutes, I was toast.

I remember going to the final for one math class that I was registered for but had never attended. The professor said, "I've never seen you before."

And I replied, "I haven't been here, but I'm ready for the test."

But as it worked out, I couldn't sustain cramming for the third semester of organic chemistry; in fact, I fell asleep during the exam. That quarter I received all Ds and Fs and the Dean called me in and said, "You're not going to class, so maybe you should take a year off."

I replied, "That's fine. I'm never coming back here."

It had to have been the shortest Dean's meeting he had ever had.

So after a year and a half at Northwestern, at nineteen, I returned home, a failure in my mother's and most of my family's eyes. I was told that I had blown the greatest opportunity of my life, and sometimes I wondered if they were right. My mother had remarried and now there were ten kids in the house. The terms for my return home, and it was a chilly welcome, was that I would cook dinner for the family and would pay rent. But that was fine with me, because I enjoyed cooking, and I even started cooking for my mom's parties.

Mark Laubacher, a good friend from Northwestern, had given me my very first cook book, on preparing Mexican food. I made friends with a nice lady at a nearby Mexican grocery store, and she helped me a lot in terms of learning the ins and outs of cooking Mexican food. I have always preferred hands-on learning. Although it's tattered and worn and has been through many moves, I still have that very first cook book.

As luck would have it, I soon had a really good job at the Chicago Stock Exchange, where I found myself making twenty grand a year, which wasn't too bad for 1979. And where some people might be put off with all of the seeming confusion and yelling at a stock exchange as stocks are bought and sold, it didn't phase me a bit. I simply got myself into the zone, and everything sorted itself out automatically.

It was during this time that I met Bryce at a party. Although we had very few things in common, we got along well and had a lot of fun. Bryce loved to go out to eat, and she introduced me to some of Chicago's best eating spots. She turned me on to Chinese food and sushi and opened my eyes to the enormous array of choices that exist in the culinary arts. In fact, after Bryce and I hooked up, I decided to leave home once again. After all, my life had been pretty much confined to Oak Park, and now it was time to discover Chicago, since I was working there each weekday at the stock exchange.

One of my buddies at the exchange was Phil, who was a former Marine who had spent two tours in Vietnam. Nobody messed with Phil because they knew he could kill them in a heartbeat, if necessary. We would go out and shoot pool on Friday and Saturday nights and play for Heineken. I was an ace at pool, and Phil would watch my back. Twice, though, guys pulled guns on me and put them up to my head. Phil would just walk up to them and tell them that they really didn't want to do that, and they would put their guns away.

My other party buddy, Pinky, who was from Oak Park, worked as a cook. He got me a job working in Chicago's fifth busiest restaurant — a Swedish restaurant that had over 200 employees — as the Sunday omelette guy. That was perfect, because I loved visiting with the customers. Pretty soon the chef offered me a full time job and I took it on the spot, leaving my position at the Chicago Stock Exchange. Bryce flipped out. She couldn't believe that I would trade my job at the stock exchange for one making $ 4.25 an hour. I kept saying to her, "But I'm a cook." Our paths soon parted.

One pays one's dues with any job, and the staff at the restaurant did their best to rough me up in my new work. They insisted, for example, that I must reach into the lobster tank to get lobsters rather than using tongs. But it didn't matter. I was home, meaning that I had found a new place where I could disappear, just the way I had disappeared sorting bottles and packing newspapers. Most athletes call this experience the zone. It certainly is magical. The process called thinking virtually dissolves, as one finds oneself in the middle of everything that is happening, but everything seems to be running itself, sort of on autopilot.

At the restaurant, I was quickly moved to lunchtime sauté, with six to eight burners going at once. Many of our customers were retired. We called them "blue hairs" — and they loved liver. In addition to cooking on all those burners, we also had to do prep work, like slicing thirty pounds of mushrooms or peeling and preparing forty pounds of shrimp. But it didn't matter; I loved what I was doing. However, one day early in my time there, I had not yet completely entered "flow" and moving too fast, I almost cut the tip of my thumb off.

The chef took me to the emergency room, and as we waited to get the required stitches, he said, "You're really into this. Have you ever thought of chef school?'

"Chef school?"I was flabbergasted. I knew of Harvard and Yale and Northwestern, but had never heard that there were schools that taught the culinary arts. And right then and there I knew not only that I had to go, but that I would soon be going.

As it worked out, my boss had taken his training at what is considered by many to be the world's finest culinary school, the Culinary Institute of America, located on the site of a former Jesuit Seminary in Hyde Park, New York. He made a couple of calls on my behalf, and his enthusiasm and support advanced me in the applicant pool, and within four months, I was on my way to the CIA.

My mom was disappointed when I dropped out of Northwestern, although for some reason my dad wasn't. He knew that I would be fine. When I discovered that I wanted to pursue culinary arts, my mom was ecstatic, for in her mind I had found solid direction for my life and career. And to my good fortune, my dad had a connection that would eventually connect me with one of my teachers.

My step-mother, my dad's new wife, was a coat check girl at Gordon's, which was at that time one of the five best restaurants in Chicago. We all lived in a little commune in a small apartment, and my step-mom invited John Terczak to come, and he showed up. I had met him once before at a place called The Smart Bar, when he had catered my dad's and step-mom's first anniversary party. Terczak was at that time *the* celebrity chef of Chicago, and during our brief visit at my going away party, he said he would have a place for me when it came time for my externship. I accepted his offer, and thought I had it made. What a dream, to be able to become an understudy to one of the greatest chefs in America!

There was much to do, and do quickly, with my relatively sudden departure for the East. I was determined not to live on campus at the Culinary Institute of America, because even the thought of doing so brought back the continual partying scenes at Northwestern before I washed out. In short, I was petrified at the prospect of *any* socializing for fear of reverting to my party self, and finding myself at the end of my culinary training.

Now, see if this can be comprehended in one reading: my mom's new husband's sister was married to a Colonel who was in charge of a huge munitions depot in New Jersey, which was only an hour or two from the CIA. And since our family would always hang together for mutual support, it was decided that I would visit the Colonel and his wife and stay with them for a week before beginning classes, and each day drive up to Poughkeepsie to look for an apartment.

So I crammed my little diesel V. W. Rabbit completely full and took to the East to seek my fortune. Just imagine what I must have looked like, chugging up to the guardhouse at the entrance of the munitions dump, like some wayward college kid looking for shelter. And to complicate my initial reception, I couldn't remember the Colonel's name, so before anyone could say Jack Lightning, I was out and up against my little Rabbit, being frisked for weapons and drugs. In my panicked state, I managed to remember the Colonel's name, at which point all of the soldiers snapped to full attention, therein immediately after extending me a three car escort to his quarters.

And each day of the following week, I would drive north in hope of finding suitable accommodations for school, but each day came home absolutely empty. Toward the end of the week, I needed to try a new approach and went into visit the *est* headquarters in New York City. My dad had gotten really involved in *est* in Chicago and had introduced me to it. My younger brother Jeff and I attended Dad's graduation from *est*. As it worked out, I went through the program's initial weekend training. It was all based on the need to 'be here now' and selfless service to others, which had always made sense to me. I can't remember a time when I didn't want to help others. And it was an entirely volunteer organization, and I soon began volunteering to help with all of the programs that were available in Chicago. One of the big things that came out of it was that I was able to cry again. I hadn't been able to cry since I was about ten or eleven. And I also got back in touch with how much I loved my mom and dad. In fact, it was at one of the *est* seminars that I had the epiphany that I wanted to become a chef.

Anyway, no sooner had I mentioned my need for a place to stay in Poughkeepsie than one of the staffers at the New York City *est* Center gave out a call to everyone in this huge room. Before I knew it, I was talking on the phone with an *est* connection who had a room available about ten miles from the CIA. It was a great relief to cut the deal on the phone, and I drove up the next day, a day before classes started.

Chuck and Sally Stark, brother and sister, lived in this house, which was one of three on a 160 acre Christmas tree farm. Chuck was a horse trainer, a real outdoors kind of guy. In fact, he'd never even visited New York City. Sally was a student a Vassar, although she was in her late twenties or so. Their house was actually a converted barn, but it was cozy and just perfect for my need. And cozy is a word that I cling to whenever I think of my January journey to that place, which sat high up on a hill and received torrents of wind.

In fact, the next morning, on January 3rd, my little Rabbit wouldn't start, and I had to wake Chuck up to tell him that I had a 7:00 a.m. class and ask him if he could take me. I remember saying, "I know you don't know me, but I really need a ride to school." Fortunately, he obliged. We found out shortly thereafter that my car needed a special oil heater tube to ensure its starting without problems on cold, windy winter mornings.

The Culinary Institute of America today sits on an eighty-acre campus that was once a Jesuit monastery, a great pile of brick and concrete with over 150 rooms. Originally, it began in New Haven, Connecticut, in 1946, but soon outgrew its facilities, ultimately moving to Hyde Park, New York in 1970. Since my days there, the CIA has considerably enlarged its campus, both in Poughkeepsie and beyond. When I was there, most of the faculty were from Europe, and we are talking about the very 'old, old' school of training, wherein teachers would think nothing of shouting or spitting or kicking. In fact, most of

30

my teachers were not very nice. The place, at that time, was super serious. Only about five percent of the student body of some 1,600 were women, and they cried most of the time. Nevertheless, the place had earned the enviable reputation as being the finest culinary school in the entire world, and I knew that I had a lot to learn.

The entire program was twenty-one months in length, including an externship of four months after the first half of the training that afforded students the opportunity to get valuable experience. A new class of thirty students would commence every four or six weeks. We would only take one class at a time, and that class could be anywhere from a week and a half up to three weeks. I really enjoyed my classes where the chefs were good teachers and cared about their students. Most chefs were not especially good teachers, however, and resorted to their harsh and old-fashioned European ways. To be sure, I got kicked in the shins and spit at in the face. One chef even called everyone 'stupid.'

My very first class involved learning how to make the five 'mother sauces' in five days. I botched one of those sauces, and when I took it up to my professor, who insisted on tasting it, I begged him just to fail me. But despite my warning, he went ahead and tasted it and suddenly got really bug-eyed and spit the sauce out and started cursing at me. Such was the rigor faced in learning from temperamental genius chefs. Wanting to immerse myself completely in my new-found calling, I soon joined every club that I could and spent my evenings reading French cookbooks. Whereas most of the students knew a lot more than I did about culinary art owing to their wider experience, my strength was in having perfected my ability to enter into 'the zone' — to disappear. On the first day in the program, I knew that before long I would be hanging with the best of them. And despite all of the adversity, a real bond formed among the various groups of students going through the program.

31

I remember how our group of thirty-two, sixteen students from the morning and sixteen from evening, set a school record when, through our persistent and collective effort, every single student passed the school's business accounting class. It had never happened before, and it was the talk of the school for a while. Culinary arts is truly one of the *arts*, and chefs really tend to be more right-brained than not. Courses like accounting can present unwanted challenges to many students who have no love or inclination to details. With my background in organic chemistry and calculus, I found it a breeze, and I was only too happy to coach my classmates and help them get over this dreaded hurdle. They would have done the same for me.

Chuck and Sally must have thought there was something wrong with me, because I always turned down their invitations to go out drinking. But I knew that school had to be on a 24/7 basis for me, or I would be back in Chicago wondering what had happened. Sally helped me by getting a Vassar library card. Even though I was abstaining from partying, I still wanted to be around women. It was enough to sit among them. I spent a lot of time in the Vassar library and also had a card for Marist College. One night I fell asleep and got locked in! When I woke up, it brought back memories of Northwestern, for the same thing had happened there a number of times. The Marist library was pitch black, but I managed to feel my way along the wall and finally reached a telephone and could call security, which was totally flabbergasted by my presence there.

On Saturday mornings, Chuck and I would make the rounds to get fresh eggs and fresh milk. We would often stop out for breakfast on those mornings. Chuck was one tough, country cowboy, and toward the end of my stay with them, I took Chuck down to New York City, where he was so flummoxed by the Big Apple, that we never emerged from the first bar we entered until it was time to go back up to

Poughkeepsie. You can take the rustic guy out of the country, but not the country out of the dude. Chuck and Sally were happily inclined to their rustic ways, and I loved being a part of their family. They had a dog that was half Alaskan malamute and half wolf. In the winter, it would bring home a deer and then eat on it for the next three days. It was trip! Chuck and Sally were good people, and I will always be grateful for their many kindnesses and will never forget them.

When my classmates were scrambling to find positions for their externships from the CIA, I thought I was set because John Terczak had offered me a position at my going away party. In fact, I tended to brag a little about it, because I couldn't believe that I would be working with one of Chicago's true master chefs. So when my externship arrived, I called Terczak to make arrangements, only to find out that he not only didn't remember me, but that he had forgotten the promise he had made! But I persisted, because I had nothing else, and he finally said to come, but that if I couldn't teach him something new in the first three days, I wouldn't have a job. I had even doubled up on some of my last month's classes so as to extend my time with Terczak.

So for two days during what I expected would become my very truncated, three-day externship, certain that I didn't have anything to show Terczak that he didn't already know. I found myself sitting in the basement of the Gordon's sister restaurant, that was right next door, pealing potatoes with Terczak's fifteen-year-old stepson who was crazier than a loon and wilder than an entire zoo. I kept thinking, "Why did I sign on for this?"

On the third day, which I expected would be my last, Terczak suddenly came in and said, "Follow me."

He led me across the alley into Gordon's small kitchen, and explained that Chino, who ran Gordon's, had not shown up for the third time and was done. The orders for dinner were beginning to come in, and Terczak showed me two two-tops and then left.

I began to fill orders as they were handed to me and looked at my two co-workers. I asked Martine Astute, who took care of the cold side, salads and desserts, "Why didn't you take this job?"

He just looked at me and said, "You'll see."

Then I looked at Johnny IDE, the grill cook, and asked him the same question, and he said, "You'll see."

I began to feel more than a little like Lucy Ricardo in that famous "I Love Lucy" show where she got a job boxing chocolates, and the chocolates kept coming out on the conveyor belt faster and faster.

And then Gordon himself walked in and looked at me, exclaiming, "Who in the hell are you and what are you doing in my kitchen?"

All I could say was, "I'm Greg, and I don't know why, and I'm really busy."

Gordon stormed out, muttering that he was going to kill Terczak.

And as unlikely as it might seem, I managed to beat all odds at Gordon's. I had a lot of sauté experience and could disappear, so that part went like clockwork. And since Martine and Johnny didn't want my job, they were kind enough to carry me for the first couple of weeks to make sure that everything worked out.

I will never forget that tiny kitchen. It was at least 120 degrees every night. It was at Gordon's that I learned the importance of drinking room temperature water and wearing my hair really short. I never passed out at my station, although one night I took a short break, and suddenly found Martine and Johnny picking me up where I had passed out on my car outside. Trust me. Cooking is not for the fainthearted. Stamina is essential, as is agility. And if one cooks with just one's sight and touch, it doesn't work. At least, it doesn't work for me. I cook with my ears, with everything. My "disappearing" allows me to do that, but

34

that doesn't mean that one isn't aware of what's happening. I had to be aware of everything that was happening. That must be why I had done so well during my short stint at the Chicago Stock Exchange.

It was at Gordon's that I realized that I could really succeed as a chef. That is where it all came together, talk about testing by fire! I was home. And home is like a connectedness where I can melt away — or where I am there in a different way — I become fully attuned to everything around me. I can almost hear the fish saying, 'I'm done.' That may sound crazy, but it's true. I remember running a two-hundred-seat restaurant in Florida where I literally knew everything that was happening, at all of the stations, even though I was at the dishwasher. When I go into the zone, or disappear, my hands warm up. I feel real safe, and I find that I no longer "think" — at least, not in the normal way. Something far better and larger replaces it, and allows everything to go smoothly and effortlessly.

After less than six weeks at Gordon's, Gordon walked in and looked at me and said, "Greg, you are the best night cook that I have ever had." In fact, he told my mom and stepfather the same thing. Gordon's had validated my calling to the culinary arts, although it was through sheer baptism by fire that I proved myself, yet I rejoiced that this venue of serving others was proving so effective — to be sure, it was a hell of a lot of work, but with my ability to disappear, that didn't really matter. Still, there was a nagging knowingness that was hard to put into words, that even though I had found a professional home, I still didn't belong. And midway through my externship at Gordon's, Terczak accepted a job at a New York City hotel, and he took me with him.

With the new venue, which I thought was great, I thought that my future in the world of culinary arts was secure. I would work at the hotel on weekends, and then full-time after graduating from the CIA. But such hopes are often dashed on the shores of circumstances beyond one's own control, and it turned out that Terczak was fired not many months after we had arrived.

But Terczak never lacked for new opportunities, and a prominent New York City restauranteur named David Kay, who was always accompanied by a body guard and who gambled a great deal, contracted with Terczak to open three restaurants. The first one was to be called Pig Heaven, which was on 81st Street and 2nd Avenue and the plan was to feature a twenty-four hour restaurant that would offer a Chinese venue for twelve hours and an American venue for twelve hours. David Kay also ran the fanciest Chinese restaurant in New York City, Auntie Juan's, and, in fact, was the one who first brought Szechuan flavors to America.

Terczak was slated to be in charge of the American venue at Pig Heaven, and Simon, who was without doubt the finest Chinese chef in the city, was assigned to the Chinese portion. And would it surprise anyone to learn that Terczak and Simon hated each other? Passions in the domain of culinary arts can run high. And shortly before the restaurant opened, there was fire in the duck oven, which is a huge walk-in oven designed to catch the fat for both ducks and pigs. And a fire in one of these ovens is like an enormous deep fryer catching on fire,

Terczak, who probably had the most experience of anyone with kitchen fires, jumped up and started putting it out. What none of us realized on the American venue side is that a fire in the kitchen of a new restaurant is considered good luck by Chinese custom, and is allowed to burn for a couple of minutes before being put out. The Chinese workers rushed to stop Terczak, who was a big, bulky, bald tattooed guy, the kind who *never* lost a fight. It was like something out of a Kung Fu movie. Terczak shouted to me, "Christian, what's happening?" But I didn't know, and so it went on.

36

Finally Simon showed up and freaked out when he found how rude we had been to the good luck fire, and he told David Kay on the spot that either Terczak went, or he would go. So David Kay announced that Pig Heaven would immediately become a completely twenty-four hour Chinese restaurant.

Thus plans were advanced where Terczak and others, including myself, would plan two new restaurants, each one with 250 seats, sharing a common kitchen, on 65th Street and 3rd Avenue. One would be called Café Marimba and the other Safari Grill. It was my distinct privilege to work with the famous French restaurant designer Sam Lopata. At the CIA, we were told that only one out of ten of us would ever have the opportunity to design a new restaurant from bottom up. And what a trip! We had a lot of custom kitchen pieces put together and had seven-walk-in coolers. In fact, we won the best kitchen design award for an American commercial kitchen in 1984.

Terczak asked me to help him with interviews, and his philosophy was to be really rough on applicants to see what they were made of. We didn't want anyone who thought he or she was his or her resume. We were looking for passionate chefs with heart, who weren't afraid to give it their all. In fact, at the beginning of the interviews, we ripped up the applicants' resumes to study their reaction. It was a valuable screening device, although not very humane. It's something I don't think I'd ever do again.

David Kay managed to get the famous foodie Eddie Shoenfeld to come and bring others to assist in developing the menus for each restaurant. And, ironically, the problem we eventually faced was our own success. Safari Grill received a favorable review from Brian Miller, and we got slammed. The problem was that the menu Terczak had devised was too complicated to get the food out on time, no matter what we did. But he wouldn't budge, and we found ourselves behind the eight ball for many months, until business finally slowed down. And I want to emphasize that the only reason we couldn't get the food out on time was that there was no way to add additional cooking stations, beyond the twenty-five already in place. For those several years, it was my distinct honor and privilege to work with and to learn from some of the finest cooks in New York City — nine of the best cooks with whom I have ever worked.

For these two restaurants, Terczak created a position for me. He hated any kind of detail and, had, in fact, never owned his own restaurant and therefore never had to be responsible for balancing budgets. Hence, I became his right-hand guy, and overseeing most details related to the on-going needs of the business. Part of my job was to make sure that everyone's station was set up properly. And Terczak always said my greatest gift was that I was somehow able to eliminate any competition around me, and trust me, there can be a hell of a lot of it in the culinary arts. No one in the restaurant, though, would ever have felt the need to be competitive with me if they knew how much Terczak paid me. I wasn't making much more than the dishwasher.

That was part of Terczak's European manner, a way of kicking down those around him, and for me, it was my pay. In fact, Terczak had the biggest ego of anyone I ever met or knew in the field of culinary arts. He also had the charisma of a cult leader, and barely needed to walk into a room before he would be surrounded by potential investors, wanting to throw money at him.

But we all have our blindspots and shortfalls. Tercsak started partying and was finally fired by David Kay. I was offered his position, but didn't want it. It felt disloyal, until someone explained that it was going to be given to someone, so why not me, since I knew all the ins and outs of the business. So I accepted. A couple of weeks later, Terczak shows up in the kitchen, glaring at me and literally shaking with anger, saying, "Christian, what are you doing?" He always called me Christian.

And I said, "Look, John. I'm sorry you lost your job, but you should have expected it to happen for not showing up and for all the partying you were doing." Terczak called me less than two months later to say he had forgiven me, and not long after that, he wanted me to come down to Washington, D.C., and assist him with a new restaurant there. And normally I might have gone, except that I already had a great gig in New York, and I also didn't think Terczak would last long in D.C.. And it turned out that I was right, and I was sad for him.

So, in 1984, just out of chef school, I found myself working one hundred hours a week, and making about sixty grand a year. Not bad for 1984, when I think of it. And what meant the most to me during those couple of years was all that I learned from the other chefs, who knew far more and had far wider experience than I had. Eliot, Mark Weisman, Dina, and Henry Bronson, whom we called the Taz, all of them — just tops, and I still remain in touch with some of them even today. Those couple of years, looking back, constituted for me my progression in the profession — it was a fun time, a time of bonding, a time of learning, a time of giving one's all.

What saved me and my sanity during those years in New York City was a place that sold time in these floatation tanks, that are designed to help people to relax. I would go religiously every Sunday afternoon for two to three hours. It let me unwind. And before long I discovered that I could actually float outside my body, first in the environs of the float tank and building, but then even outside the building. This discovery brought back memories of things I had long forgotten. One was that, when younger, probably about ten or so, I was able to float outside of my body. It happened regularly when my dad had his band over for parties — a time when music and love and well-being filled the air and permeated the entire house. I noticed that my body would get warm all over and that I would feel surrounded by the all-encompassing joy and euphoria. I loved those parties, and I would find myself out of body and invisible to others and simply floating down the back hallways of the house. I would wake up in my bed the next morning. For some reason, it never happened at our family holiday parties, but only with dad's musician friends.

I realize now that my ability to leave my body and to enter the zone are really the same thing. It took me to a peaceful, loving place, where normal thinking would abate and anything I was doing would simply and effortlessly proceed. My nickname in New York was One Match, for I never needed more than one match to get a wood burning fire going perfectly. But, looking back, I wasn't the master of fire that I may have fancied; it was the zone, or what miraculous abilities that flowed through it, that allowed me to give the best of all that I was to whatever I was doing.

Yet that inner nagging voice continued, the voice that doubted that I had really arrived. That I was an up and coming chef was apparent and clear to everyone but myself. I may have found a professional home, but I still didn't feel as if I belonged. Maybe I lacked real confidence deep down inside, or maybe I didn't have the resilient ego that most chefs seem to need. All I knew was that part of me didn't belong, and I had to hide that, for fear that someone might find out. So after a year of solo work in New York, I decided to return to Chicago.

Chapter Four
Light Out of Darkness

LITTLE DID I KNOW when I returned to Chicago that I would soon begin five of the most challenging years of my life, in part for what I would gain and especially for what I would lose.

Even when I reflect on those years today, I find that most of my memories have become blurred. Perhaps that is as it should be. Life certainly is not linear, so why should memory be — or even a memoir?

My dad and his second wife, Elizabeth, invited me to live with them when I returned from New York, and the second day that I was home, my dad sat me down and asked, "Where's the Greg I used to know? Who are you and where's my son?" In my time away, I had become completely hyper, ungrounded, and ever increasingly intense. In short, I was a real treat to have around. Running the kind of operation that I did in New York, especially at so young an age, had required me to be at the top of my game on a 24/7 basis.

I realized at that moment that I didn't want to work — couldn't work — but simply wanted to stay at home and meditate and eat vegetables so that I could get back into my body. My time in New York had also taught me that I didn't really want to work for other people. My daily rhythm soon included going running every night as well as dancing at the Smart Bar that was not too far from where we lived, where my nickname was Bouncy, because of the way I danced. I dabbled in the restaurant business a bit, but after half a year of unsuccessfully trying to secure financial backing for my own restaurant, I decided to get into selling commercial water filters. Everybody was selling them! I soon shared an office with Linda Stevens. We had a lot of fun, but didn't really make any money during that year, although we managed to survive. We did close a good deal with a chain, the Eagle Food Stores, as well as with an investment group, which wanted us to install a whole bunch of machines into grocery stores for five percent of the company. We were new to the business world and didn't know how to respond to that. Looking back, we might have done it under better circumstances. Mostly, I wanted to get behind something that I cared about and loved, and the only thing that had ever captured me in that way was culinary art. I suppose that it was inevitable that I would return to the kitchen sooner or later. As it worked out, it was sooner.

There is an old expression, that when the student is ready, the teacher appears. For me, that teacher was the late Michael Short. Although he did not enjoy the same limelight in which Terczak basked, he was, in my opinion, one of the great genius chefs in America. He could eat something from *any* culture and proceed to reproduce it exactly. He had a photographic memory, and he could remember *everything* he had ever made, and could reproduce it whenever he liked. One of his passions was collecting old motorcycles. Sadly, like all of us, he also had a downside, perhaps because of a dark side, and was a heroin addict and alcoholic.

He once told me, "Most people have kids to feed their egos." Whether that is true or not, I do not know. I do know that Short had a vasectomy when he was eighteen, but I have often wondered whether that was because he was afraid of the responsibility in caring for a child, mostly because he couldn't really take care of himself, and he knew it.

I had eaten at Short's restaurant, the Star Top Café, and greatly admired what was offered up there, both for its taste as well as its originality. For those first six months after I returned from New York, as I grounded myself again, I enlisted the help of Carol Blomstrand, a very reliable realtor, to search for potential places where I could open my own restaurant, provided that I could find sufficient financing. She

42

reported to me, in her search, that she had learned that Short's restaurant was quietly on the market, but that the owners didn't want anyone to know, lest the knowledge that their café might close would panic its regulars and drive them away.

Michael Short was a big drinker who would sometimes frequent the Smart Bar where I, at that time, was a big dancer where I would go almost every night. When he next showed up, I remembered what Carol had told me and also about how impressed I was with what Short could do with food, and I decided at that moment that I wanted to get back into the kitchen so that I could learn everything I could from him before he sold his restaurant and retired. I didn't want to miss an opportunity to learn from such a master of culinary art. As quiet as I may have been growing up in a parochial school, when it came to culinary art, I could become very bold. Short didn't know who I was, but I certainly knew him.

As he stood at the bar, I walked up behind him and said, "Hey, I heard that you're selling your restaurant."

He lunged around as he pulled out a switchblade from his pocket and held it against my throat and demanded, "Who told you that?"

I wasn't afraid of him and just looked at him and told him to put the switchblade away. He started to laugh as he pocketed his knife and we began to talk. I told him who I was and that I wanted to work for him. He told me that he couldn't pay me what I was worth, but that was just fine with me. Culinary art for me has never been about the money. So I was suddenly back in the kitchen, at the Star Top Café, a small and wild storefront restaurant of fifty seats that spun old LPs, like Led Zepplin, and drew the musicians from the city's finest rock bands as well as their promoters. A lot of hipsters with money like Jerry Michaelson showed up regularly, the kind of dudes who knew good food but who also craved the loud, zany atmosphere for which the restaurant was famous.

And it all worked because Short was the kind of genius who cooked with great abandon. All of the rules of French cooking were followed, while at the same time none of the rules were followed! All rules — no rules. It was the classic interplay between the intellect and intuition, and it spawned the most imaginative and delectable dishes. An ironic fact is that Michael Short and John Terczak had studied with the same teacher, a chef who ran what was called the Dumas Pere Cooking School somewhere in Chicagoland — I think it may have been in Glencoe, Illinois, but I'm not sure. The chef who ran the school was truly nuts, which may explain the later behavior of both Short and Terczak. In fact, the chef had lost four of the fingers on both of his hands when they got shot off during a struggle with a would-be robber. Fingers or not, their teacher reportedly could do anything, but was a nutty drinker on top of all that. Anyway, Short couldn't afford the school and became the teacher's assistant to help pay his way. Needless to say, Michael Short and John Terczak hated each other. The universe blessed me with two master chefs for my most important teachers, and I loved them both and I learned more from them than I can ever recount in words. Nevertheless, their persistent drug addictions, habits that mirrored my own alcoholism, pushed me to the very limits of anything that might be considered sane or healthy.

I loved and cherished every minute of that first interval when I was able to work at Michael Short's Star Top Café — six days a week, for the better part of a year. We had a small, two-person kitchen, and my co-cook was Catherine August; we complemented each other perfectly, although our cooking styles were totally different. I liked showing up an hour or two early, so that I could get all my stuff in place and then treat myself to a meal of some great tastes; Catherine preferred to work on an adrenaline rush and would always show up at the very last minute, so much so that she often needed to ask Jose, our dishwasher, to help her in some of her prep work. And he was good; in fact, he ended up becoming a rock star cook. Short usually woke up around 2:00 p.m., having caroused all night, and would be hung over until about 6:00 p.m.. We would go into the cooler each day and then write the menu by hand, for it was never the same. It all depended on what was available to cook. Not long after I started working for him, Michael Short told me that I was the best cook with whom he had ever worked, certainly high praise from someone of his talent. The energy of the café was unbelievably and wonderfully open-hearted. For all of its lack in external organization, it overflowed with creativity. Bill Ammons, the cafe's co-owner, and Ellie waited on tables. Those of us in the kitchen would occasionally turn the restaurant's one clock ahead by about fifteen minutes, and call Bill's attention to it when he walked by, and he would say, "Wow! We're really running late. We need to close." We didn't do it that often, and we taught Jose how to turn it ahead and turn it back. It was great fun.

It was at the Star Top Café that I learned that the customer is not always right. Short was crazy, and had little tolerance for customers who got out of line. For example, a new customer, all dressed up and with a fancy car and gorgeous date, would tell Short that the music was too loud. Short would say, "Can I talk to you outside?" They would step outside, at which time Short would start pummeling the guy, with his date eating her dessert and suddenly looking up and going nuts.

During my first summer at Star Top, my job was to roast whole animals in the backyard next to the kitchen, as well as to rack cue balls for customers who wanted to play pool outside. Short and Ammons were really fine pool players and even took lessons and had their own special cues. What they didn't know, however, was that I had become an ace at pool over the years. I probably could have put myself through college by playing pool if I had stayed at Northwestern. One night Short asked me if I wanted to play him, and I kicked his ass. Dumbfounded, he growled, "Why didn't you say you could play pool?" I answered, "You never asked."

As I mentioned before, Short was more than kind of crazy around the edges. People tend to think of us as professionals, chefs or cooks, and that is certainly what we are. But we have all won distinguished training in the culinary *arts*, and we are artists, and that artistic temperament is very deeply ingrained in all of us, especially when it comes to food preparation and the environs in which it is made. After Short completed his training at the Dumas Pere Cooking School, he sought additional training from some of Chicago's fanciest chefs, including Jean Joho and Michael Foley.

Whenever Short became convinced that he had learned all that he could learn from somebody, he'd walk. He'd just walk out that very day, no notice, nothing, thank you very much. Although with Michael Foley, it was a little different, perhaps because Foley is a total screamer, the kind of petulant chef you sometimes see on television and wish you hadn't. The day that Short decided to walk out on Foley, he surreptitiously tied Foley's apron to the kitchen's Ansell fire suppressant system, the kind that releases the finest of mists to extinguish any fire. Such a release shuts down a restaurant for at least a couple of days for the necessary and arduous cleanup. And Short decided to walk out on Foley on a Friday, and a whole weekend's business was completely lost.

I would not trade that year of working at Michael Short's Star Top Café for anything. I loved working for him, for the challenges, the creativity, and the joy. But I had also had to provide for my wife Edita and our newborn daughter Aja and I needed a lot more money than Michael could give me, and so as it happened, John Terczak had returned to Chicago to open a new restaurant. I don't know how John managed to do what he did. His mere presence was like magic, and he no sooner could walk into a room than he would have all the big money guys throwing all their resources his way. He never had a problem getting financing in Chicago. Anyway, he had hired some good cooks but was having trouble getting the systems into place, so he hired me as a consultant. As brilliant as a chef as John is, he never did very well with the nuts and bolts of running a restaurant. For me, maybe because of my strong background in math and science, it was easy. Calculating food costs, checking on inventory, and arranging schedules was a cinch.

But, as I was to discover, I had reunited for what would be six months with the same old Terczak. Typically, his menu was once again much too complicated for too small a kitchen and too few cooks. Everybody was always behind. Normally it doesn't take more than four or five moves to make an entree, but with Terczak's menu, you were lucky if you could turn out the dish with only ten moves. Of course, the customers liked it, but they didn't have to see the huge number of pots and pans in the kitchen with everybody scrambling to keep up.

So I was called in as Terczak's consultant to help him get his house in order. Jack Jones, the head chef, was doing great and I did my best to fill in all the holes, while reassuring him that I was definitely not after his job. Looking back at how well Terzac and I had complemented each other, I knew then and know today that we could have shared a culinary empire together, except for our addictive personalities that inevitably caused us to fail. Unfortunately, the partying had gotten more frequent and he was disappearing for a couple of days at a time. Worst of all, he had begun to party with some of the cooks, and then, because he thought it was fun, gambling with them on their pay day and winning their money back. This, of course, bred justified resentment and the cooks started to take advantage of him, stealing stuff out the back door and treating him with disrespect and, in general, having their way with his restaurant.

So, wanting to help my friend and mentor, I confronted him, and said that whatever he wanted to do with his habit was entirely up to him, but that he shouldn't fraternize with the staff in that way, because they had lost respect for him and were robbing him blind. But Terczak didn't want to hear that. He fired me the next day. It was just one week before Christmas, 1990. I couldn't believe it. I said to him, "John, I was the best man at your wedding. I'm like your brother. Are you sure that you want to do this?" And he was sure or, perhaps, it is more accurate to say that his habit was sure. I knew then that the empire I had envisioned could never be built. I also knew that Terczak, like me, had chosen his habit and would be at its mercy.

Ironically, two years ago, seventeen years later, Terczak called me out of the blue and asked me to forgive him for firing me. I had gotten over it years ago. At first I didn't know what he was talking about. He was calling from Florida, proclaiming, "Christian, I'm like a whale in a bathtub in this city." Normally, I don't challenge people. I was out there partying for twenty years myself, and I always got mad when people would make challenging remarks. But I was at the end of my patience and asked, "John, why don't you sober up and stay sober so you can start helping people for change?" My hope was that John would be able to find his way back to Chicago. There are only a few as great as John Terczak.

Can you imagine what it is like to be fired from your job one week before Christmas? And to have no money? And a wife and daughter? How do you support your family on no money? Edita did her best to get unemployment compensation, but we didn't qualify. She became so nervous in the unemployment line that she dropped Aja and called me in a panic to come and get them. Losing my income was painful enough, but I also had to listen to Edita's worried litany, "You promised me that everything would be okay, and now we don't have any money. You promised me!"

My salvation was that I was able to go back to work for Michael Short at the Star Top Café. In fact, after a most meager and extremely subdued Christmas, I was able to work at the café on New Year's Eve, little knowing the depth of sorrow that 1991 was ringing in for me and my family. Edita and I would manage financially; the sorrow that was coming would not come from material loss but rather from the loss of loved ones, with one loss anticipated and the other one completely out of the blue.

To make up for our financial shortfall, I was forced to look for another job and was lucky to find one working in prep for a catering company, which, ironically, opened new doors and vistas that I had never before even imagined. I had absolutely no idea what catering was and just needed a job to make some extra money. And it turned out to be in the home kitchen of the caterer who hired me. The prep work was easy, and I was really grateful to have the job. One day, however, a call came in from our event site. They had run short of something — I forget exactly what it was, napkins or chicken or something like that — and they asked me to take whatever it was that was needed over to the Park West. When I got there, I walked into this huge event set up for five hundred people, and was greeted by Andy Lawrence, who was the captain for that event. Andy is a cool guy, and he said, "Welcome to the show!" I began to look around and took everything in at lightning speed, and suddenly realized, "I could do this. I really could. In fact, I want to."

You've got to be really fluid if you take things on the road. How it works is that you show up two or three hours before the event starts. A truck pulls up and they hand you a menu. Then they introduce you to your team and give you the time line and food and say, "Go!" It could be a party for fifty or five hundred. It could be in a fancy, formal ballroom or out in the middle of the woods. They unload the truck and set up your pretend kitchen. You may have electricity or not. You may have water or not. Each event is its own adventure! I got it, and I liked it. And within a few months I became a "star" party chef, which was a good thing, because things were really winding down at the Star Top Café; in fact, it was finally sold. So I was able to work a whole lot of parties for the lady who first hired me, and then put myself out as an independent contractor and worked for ten different caterers.

Professionally speaking, I knew I was that home once again, that I belonged. I realized that I could shine in catering, because I don't panic, just like the time that lady ran over my foot when I was ten. I screamed once and was done. And I went into catering confident that I could become one of the best caterers in Chicago. My attitude was and is: "One day I'm going to get my ass kicked in catering, but *not* today." I soon became totally absorbed in what seemed to me to be a new, wonderful and exciting universe.

But then the very bottom of my world dropped out. It fell out at 8:00 p.m. on July 17, 1991, when the police called. Edita and I were having a small dinner party at home with two friends. The police wouldn't give any information over the phone, which is never a good sign, but they finally said to me, "You've got to come to the hospital right now. Your brother Jeff is still alive."

Jeff was five years younger than me and we had always shared a room when we were kids. During those years of sharing we had forged a special bond. He was the most sensitive of any of us kids and he certainly bore the brunt of our parents' dysfunctional marriage. He was at that age when he needed the most reassurance and attention, and got the least. The upshot of it was that he took refuge in acting out, and I

50

mean really acting out. The extremes he went to seek attention only emphasized how starved he was for love.

Jeff had been driving down the street on his motorcycle and passing a parked UPS truck when a car shot out from nowhere, sending him flying off his bike as he struck it. He never regained consciousness, but he lingered for ten days. We slept in the hospital every night. My mom and dad were now together for the first time in twenty years. The head injury that Jeff sustained from the accident caused his brain to expand, until we finally had to unplug him from the respirator since there was no hope for his recovery. But even the thought that we might have to unplug Jeff was abhorrent to me, something tougher than I ever thought I'd have to face. An endless tape loop running in my head and I just couldn't get myself to say "unplug" my brother. He was only twenty-six.

Can you imagine anything that could ever be tougher than making such a decision? But then the in-fighting started between whether he would be buried or cremated. Dad took over and decided that we were going to bury Jeff, and all of my siblings signed a petition against it, since Jeff had expressed his wish to some of them that he be cremated. They came to me and I said that since nothing was in writing, we should follow our dad's direction. You would think that at a time like that, a family would come together. Ours, as it worked out, went the other way. It took years for everyone to get over it. Mom and Dad finally got together for a meal over Christmas last year. Our family was always fractured and dysfunctional; unfortunately, Jeff's death only served to deepen those fractures.

I was working for a lot of different caterers at the time of Jeff's accident, and it was ironic that my work during those ten hospital days was at the Chicago Rehabilitation Institute, just across the street. I was grateful to be able to get out of the hospital room. Maybe it was my denial, but I just couldn't sit there and look at Jeff lying in the bed on a respirator and all kinds of tubes coming and going. As Jeff's condition deteriorated, I thought more and more about the life we had shared.

Jeff was very bright and probably what we would today call dyslexic. And as I mentioned earlier, he also got the least attention of any of us kids, but was the one who needed it the most. Consequently, he acted out. He was stealing cereal from warehouses when he was ten and keeping the stash in his room. My mother never asked him anything, because I don't think she really wanted to know. He would often share his sugar cereal with us, and sometimes not. He was lighting fires at ten, and not just one garbage can — he'd go for the whole street. By eleven he was climbing up the most uninviting trees and structures and hanging from them, including hanging over busy highways. Essentially, Jeff did what Jeff did. End of story. But the law caught up to him, and he was almost taken away from our family.

All of our Italian relatives were really tough on him, and all he could hear from our mother was, "Why can't you be like your brother?" Such recurrent recriminations certainly cast me in the unenviable role of Mr. Responsible. Jeff barely finished high school and shortly thereafter took off for Europe where he worked in restaurants in Eastern Europe and sold water melons on naked beaches in Greece. He knew how to hustle, and he proved that he could take care of himself. I was in New York City at the time, and we began writing back and forth. In my letters, I encouraged him to dare to be what would make him happy, and he finally decided that he wanted to become a physical therapist assistant. So he moved back to Chicago to begin his training. I found out later that he had saved all of my letters, that they had afforded him a kind of affirmation that had made a world of difference.

As I mentioned before, Jeff was the most sensitive of us kids. He could feel others' pain, both that of people and of animals. My mom's second husband, Dr. Tom Duffy, went to medical school in Mexico, and one time we all went down there for a vacation. We decided to attend a bull fight and no sooner had it started, than Jeff had to leave. He walked all the way back to our hotel. None of us really knew what a bull fight was, that it is really the slow slaughtering of a drugged animal. I'm glad that Jeff left. I wish I had left, too.

Jeff would have been a superb physical therapist assistant. He was a healer. He had so much to offer the world. And he loved kids. I'm so grateful that he was able to have a little time with Aja, our oldest daughter. The night Jeff died, after ten days of lingering in the hospital, I couldn't sleep. I just wanted to cry and let my grief out. Edita was cradling me, wanting to comfort me. But I didn't want that. I just wanted to cry and cry and cry. I kept thinking, "It should have been me." I had already seen the birth of a child, Jeff deserved that much and a lot more. But I didn't then have the tools or knowledge to be able to tell Edita how I was feeling and what I needed, and that I didn't want to be touched, that I only wanted to grieve, to let go. Edita didn't understand, but it wasn't really her fault, but rather my own inability to communicate.

In fact, it was an egregious miscommunication that marked the very beginning of our relationship. Edita and I first met at the Smart Bar in 1987. I was selling water filters during the day, meditating regularly, and running to the Smart Bar each night to dance the night away. As I reconnected with myself, my desire for the companionship of women returned. There is an etiquette to the one-night stand, and I knew it, and I did it well. The Smart Bar was an excellent place to find partners. But when I first saw Edita at the Smart Bar, I couldn't breathe. I was in awe, and I may even have physically grabbed my heart, just to have caught a of glimpse of her. I purposely stayed away from her for six months. There was no reason to talk to this person who took my breath away. I knew I didn't want to have a fleeting relationship with this woman, but every time I saw her, I felt a huge, magnetic pull that I resisted.

Finally, one night I mustered my courage and introduced my buddy Scary Perry to Edita's friend, Tina, and they went away together, but before doing so, Tina whispered in my ear that Edita would like to sleep with me. But I didn't want that. I wanted something more. But I didn't want to miss my opportunity to meet her, so I went up to her and asked her if she would like to come home with me. If looks could kill, I wouldn't be writing this memoir today. I'll never forget that indignant glare that shouted, "How dare you!"

I took immediate retreat and refuge in the company of Jill, a good friend and one of the bartenders. She had some amazing tatoos all over her body, including the word "pork" on the inside of her lip. We started walking around the bar together. I knew all the staff at Joe Shanahan's. And as we walked around, we stumbled on Edita making out with Jill's boyfriend. Jill went ballistic and it almost got into a physical fight. Finally, everyone went their separate ways. I followed Edita and apologized, and asked her if she would please consider going out on a date. With great reluctance, she gave me her number. For the next two months, it was very, very slow. We would meet at a neutral place for half an hour or so, each coming in our own car. After a couple of months, I said that I really wanted to sleep with her, but would wait for her timing. She replied that no one had ever said that to her before.

Edita worked at what was then the fanciest Sushi restaurant in the Midwest. I would go and sit outside the place for hours, just waiting until right before it closed. Then I would go in and say that I was just driving by and was hungry. Edita and I finally started to sleep together, but she was freaked out that I lived with my dad and stepmom. That made her very uncomfortable. However, the first night that I slept at her house, it turned out that she and her sister and I all slept in the same bed! In the morning, after her sister had gone to work, Edita said no one else was home. So when I got up, I went to take a shower and left the door unlocked behind me. Suddenly, this old Filipino guy walks in and looks up. It was her dad, and each of our eyes bugged out, just like you see the cartoons. I ran out of the bathroom and into Edita's room and got my pants on and ran out of the house with no shoes, socks, or shirt. It was winter, and I almost froze to death getting home.

We just eased into dating, and then Edita moved in with me and got pregnant a year later. Her dad and my mom really wanted us to get married, even though that was not what we wanted. They kept up the pressure and, finally, when Edita's dad brought a long white wedding gown home for her from Filene's Basement, Edita said, "That's it. We're going to get married." At the time, she was pregnant again with Britha, and we went to City Hall for our formal ceremony. I guess we had just gotten weary of fighting her dad and my mom and acceded to their wishes.

All in all, we had a good marriage, at least, as good as it could be. We hosted lots of dinner parties, laughed a lot together, and enjoyed our two daughters. We made a lot of trips up to Canada to visit Edita's relatives. They were all sincere and kind and fun to be with, and ninety-five percent of our shared family time was with them. I came to realize that I actually liked them as much as my own family. When we finally had a little money, Edita and I also treated ourselves to a two week trip to France. After a week in the country, our week in Paris was like the one you read about in the fantasy books, a time of love where you sleep late and then stumble into a museum or restaurant. One special time, when Edita was helping me to get dressed up as Santa Claus for her Canadian family, we were in the bathroom fumbling with the costume and we started laughing and just couldn't stop.

Edita and I are the kind of people who need all the doors to be open, who resist any kind of boundaries. That's why we never had any interest in getting married. My alcoholism couldn't have been easy for her, but I had worked through that and was sober. Most of it was that we had just stopped spending time together. She would watch a lot of television and I would hang out with my friends. When I raised the prospect of our separating, she initially disagreed, but eventually went along with it. Now we're getting along better than ever.

When I fondly remember the trips Edita and I and our kids took up to Canada, I am reminded of the two trips that my family took to Colorado when I was growing up. I'm sure that you can imagine the

56

kind of fighting that would envelope the car, with us six kids flailing around at each other, with the noise gradually rising to an unbearable pitch. Finally, we'd come up for air and discover that Dad had pulled off the road. With remarkable patience, he was looking at us all through the rear view mirror and would quietly say, "Whenever you're all done, we'll continue." How I loved those trips!

In the wake of Jeff's death, Dad and I decided that we needed to make a pact that we would not wallow in self-pity or to fall into depression so that we would ourselves become burdens to our loved ones. We decided to go back to Colorado, to the mountains, where we could cry and drink some beer together. I remember that my dad's fancy girlfriend at that time had to stop and get a hair dryer on our way. To me, it seemed a little prissy; I mean, why does anyone need a hair dryer in the mountains?

We took the trip to Colorado within a couple of weeks of Jeff's funeral, which had itself been very heart-rending. I remember seeing Michael Short and Bill Ammons at the beginning of the service, but not afterward. They later told me the service was just too intense, with all the emotion and crying, and they just couldn't stay. My dad was my best friend, always. I know he felt guilty over not having been home very much during the time when Jeff needed him most. He was ever increasingly away on tour before the divorce. We shared our regrets and mourned our dashed hopes, especially those for Jeff. Everyone in the family had begun to say, "Jeff's going to make it. He went to Europe with no money and lasted for two years. He's fearless." And he was doing really well in preparing for his career as a physical therapist assistant. Then, he was gone. So, in Colorado, out of our grief for Jeff and out of respect for our loved ones, Dad and I pledged to continue to work and to keep things going, for the sake of the family and, of course, for ourselves.

57

After Dad and I returned from our trip to Colorado, where we had made our covenant and mourned Jeff, I received news that Michael Short had died of an overdose in New Orleans. It was an exclamation point on all that had happened during those five years. When the Star Top Café closed, Short went to Florida to visit his father before moving to New Orleans. When I heard where he had gone and where he was going, I knew he had decided to hang it up. How long it would take for him to OD was anybody's guess. On the day he died the world lost one of its most eccentric and creative chefs, and I lost a dear friend and mentor. Working for him was the second best thing that happened to me during those five terrible, fantastic, wonderful, horrible years. The worst thing that happened, of course, was my brother's unexpected and untimely death. Jeff was one of the sweetest, tenderest souls that I have ever known, and I sometimes wonder how he managed to hang on as long as he did in this harsh and unforgiving world.

The very best thing that happened to me during those five years was meeting and marrying Edita and our having Aja. Ironically, it was during our trip to Colorado to mourn Jeff's death that Britha was conceived. I wish Jeff could have known her, too. He was very fond of Aja. I wish Jeff could have lived a full and productive life and could have gotten married and had his own kids. His death caused me to wonder anew about the meaning of my life as well as about the meaning of life in general. My discovery of the field of catering had brought to me, for the first time in my culinary arts career, a real sense of belonging in a professional way. At the same time, I became acutely aware of a yearning to belong, in an even deeper way, a yet unsatisfied yearning with which I had struggled my entire life.

Chapter Five
Belonging, At Last

HAVE YOU EVER FELT THAT YOU DIDN'T BELONG? I have. In fact, I have felt that way most of my life. And have you ever asked yourself, what does it really mean to belong, anyway?

In the wake of Jeff's death in late July 1991, a new self-honesty was attempting to nudge itself into my life, and I was beginning to acknowledge to myself, and only to myself, that I am an alcoholic. It was a problem that I had struggled with since I was seventeen. Reflecting back, I now see that Jeff's death afforded me a chance to reappraise myself and my life. I also understand that I unconsciously resisted that nudging by throwing myself into ninety-plus hour work weeks, deliberately seeking both refuge and escape in my catering work and in my position of teaching culinary arts at Wright College. Needless to add, I also took daily refuge in the bottle.

It would take another twelve years before I could admit to myself *and to others* that I had a problem with drinking. I am the tenacious type and have always wanted to have my own way. Or, stated more precisely, my *addiction* has always wanted to have its way with things, and it was my *addiction* that always got its way. I would work from six in the morning until midnight during those years. But I was proud of the contribution that I was making, especially in teaching the kids at Wright College. Part of the joy I discovered at Wright came from the fact that half of each class was always comprised of kids with disabilities and that they were doing their best to acquire skills that would assist them in finding jobs. My work with them showed me how much patience that I really have. Prior to that, I frequently tended to be impatient, both with my employees as well as with my children.

Whenever any of the kids graduated from the school, I always insisted that our family attend, even though Edita didn't enjoy going to the ceremonies.

The culinary arts program at Wright was comprised of a ten week program. I wrote a competency-based curriculum that ensured that no students could cut an onion before they mastered cutting a carrot, just as they could not make asparagus soup until they had demonstrated full competency in making chicken soup. We usually had a total of twenty students in each program. We were responsible for serving about one hundred and fifty hot lunches each day. From Monday through Friday, I would arrive shortly before six in the morning and check on everyone to make sure that the food was being prepared properly. And since it was a competency-based program, after the first week, everyone — and I mean *everyone* — was in a different place and going at a different speed. I was like one of those chess masters who walks around playing thirty games all at the same time.

I could never have handled the teaching position and my catering business if I had not had an assistant who took care of all of the administrative details. I invented the job and sold the school on the need for it, and I'm grateful they agreed, for I really loved the satisfaction and pleasure I received from working with those kids.

At eleven-thirty during the weekdays, I would jump in the funny little station wagon that I had bought from Carl Berman, who owned a bar called At the Tracks, out of which we catered. I'll never forget that car. You needed a screwdriver to start it. Anyway, I would race to Carl's to begin my catering work. Robert Chapin, who had worked at Carl's bar as a night cook, became my right-hand man in the catering work. He did all the prep work and washed all the dishes. If I needed more help, I could always bring in cooks like the brothers Danato and Martin Cruz. I really had no employees in the traditional sense. So I had to buy all the food, cook it, and serve it. I usually didn't get home until at least midnight, and sometimes even later, especially if I decided to go to a bar to play pool. If so, then all bets were off.

I have always been lucky. I seem to fall into just the right situations at the right time. After I had teamed up to do catering work with a woman named Lynn who had established herself with Carl Berman, she told me that she would soon be getting married and would be moving to California, and that I should talk to Carl about taking over the business. All she asked for a buyout was that I take her out for lunch to the best Sushi place in Chicago, which I did. When I asked Carl if I could continue on my own, he said, "Let's try it. Let's see if it works."

What I learned, and it may be that Carl already knew this, is that high-end catering is all about relationships, expectation and trust. Lynn had established herself with her customers, who didn't know me from Adam. In fact, they probably would have preferred to hire Adam, if they had been given the choice. As I attempted to invite them to continue with me, I kept getting very tentative responses, which, really, were tantamount to "No's." Jam Productions was Lynn's biggest account and was the very last one that I contacted. By this point, I was totally stressed out, and didn't know what I would do if my last option fell through.

Jam Productions is a prestigious concert management company that handles some of the biggest entertainers who visit Chicago. They also owned Park West, a perfect catering venue that can accommodate between two hundred to five hundred people. Jerry Michelson, one of Jam Production's owners, was a frequent patron at Michael Short's Star Top Café. Jerry loved the atmosphere and food there. And the Star Top was a place where the chefs would often take the dishes to the diners' tables and visit with them a bit. So I knew Jerry, and he knew me. When I went to meet with Jam Productions' subsidiary, Donna Sue

Fish and a guy named Scotty were very tentative. It was sort of like, "Well, we'll think about giving you a shot at it some day."

As my good luck would have it, Jerry happened to walk in and saw me and snuck up behind me and put his knees against the back of mine, so mine suddenly buckled. I whirled around in surprise and he asked me, "What are you doing here?"

I explained to him that I was trying to get their catering contract.

Jerry looked at the others and announced, "This is the guy. THIS is the guy." I know he often likes to tell others that he helped me to get my start in the field, and he certainly did, and I will be forever grateful to him for his confidence and kindness. His company started calling and the best thing about it was that all of the parties were for between two hundred and five hundred people. Jam Productions' contract certainly helped to secure my foundation in catering. In Chicago, it really helps to get catering gigs on more than just weekends, which is usually all that beginning caterers manage to do.

So my life exclusively became nothing but my career and building my company and it was non-stop. I would be racing from early morning, arriving at Wright College by six, supervising there and then doing catering stuff in the afternoon and evenings, and getting home past midnight or even later. On Sundays, I would simply plant myself on the couch all day and veg out watching sports, claiming, "I'm a sports guy. The game's on. I need my down time."

By the end of my second year of catering, there was enough business to stop teaching and to dedicate all of my time on growing the business. The guy who replaced me at Wright College changed the program and it foundered after ten weeks. I was sorry to see it go, as it had helped a lot of kids get jobs. My replacement just couldn't play as many chess games as were required.

When my business expanded, I asked Carl if I could just pay him rent and use his facilities. He agreed, saying that, "You've been honest with me and I've made some money. Go for it." Of course, that meant getting my own liquor license and business license and all that. During the first couple of years in catering, I managed to meet a large number of the city's caterers, including Wendy Adelson. We liked each other and got along well, and she was already established, and we struck a deal that she would do the business stuff and sales and that I would produce the contracted events, menus, food, and so on. We also agreed that after we had earned enough money we would build a kitchen downtown to which she would move her home office. Communication, however, became a challenge, because in high-end catering, details change, sometimes by the minute. You've got to be really fluid to succeed. If not, you're toast. You also need to have a staff in tuxes that knows what it's doing, with all the silver trays, fine wine glasses, and serving dishes, and so on.

So I built the kitchen we had talked about, but Wendy didn't want to move downtown. She finally did, but in the process we discovered that our ideas for growing the new business were radically different. In our second year, we did about three quarters of a million dollars in business, but I only took home about forty thousand dollars. My goal was to get a house for Edita and the kids and not have to rely on a relic of a car that required a screwdriver every time you started it. I also didn't want to work for *other* caterers when I had my own business, and that was something that I was forced to do to pay the bills. I was able to buy her out, and in November of 1996, my new company was incorporated as Greg Christian Catering.

The best thing that happened to me in those first couple of years of catering was meeting Hollis Haxby, who was without peer *the* caterer of the entire Midwest between 1990–2000. Hollis had worked for Chicago

Caterers, from which she had received some sweat equity. After the founder died, the company was purchased. Hollis didn't have a non-compete clause in her contract, and managed to walk away with her ten top customers. As I said before, high-end catering is all about relationships, expectation and trust. Hollis needed someone to produce the events that she would organize and plan, and she invited me to her apartment for lunch to discuss the possibility of our working together. That was sometime during the summer of 1994. Anyway, we both got drunk over a couple of bottles of wine and Hollis made me lunch and finally said, "I like you. You are my new caterer."

I said, "But you haven't even seen what I can do yet."

She responded, "No, no, no. I like you. You are my new caterer."

Suddenly I found myself catering to the top CEOs in the major Chicago companies — private dinner parties at their homes. These were events where absolutely *nothing* could go wrong. That is what was expected, and that is what we did our best to deliver. While the upside of my new job was catering to the elite power brokers of Chicago, the downside was having to work with Hollis. More than merely difficult, she would, on every event, go nuts at the very beginning. Some people need to be up against the wall for their adrenaline to kick in, so that they can solve a problem before the world ends. Hollis was like that, and she would never give us *all* of the information before an event, never saying *exactly* what she wanted. We only got about ninety-five percent of what we needed to know. I realize now, looking back, that her tantrums may have been a defense mechanism, allowing her to appease her worry and to retain control over her workers.

Whatever she perceived to be wrong was always easily fixable, especially by me; that is one of my enduring strengths. I stand strong in the face of danger or threat and I don't lose my cool. I just solve the problem, end of story. At the beginning of almost all of our events,

Hollis would begin to spin and then go nuts, engaging in her predictable tantrum all red-faced and huffing and puffing. Furthermore, she would refuse to tell me what was wrong. Her mini-rages certainly robbed the joy of having done an outstanding job, both from myself and my co-workers. But she didn't really care. And she didn't care whether or not I made my money on an event, as long as she did. She also did not want me to talk to any of our clients. Whenever she saw me visiting, she would make a bee-line over to me to listen to what we were discussing. She must have thought I was going to try to take her business away.

As difficult as those working conditions were, I also need to acknowledge a debt of gratitude to Hollis. She taught me an enormous amount about high-end catering. Hollis was a genius at finding unique ways to create a menu, table setting — sufficiently different and fresh that her clients always loved what she did. They loved her and the many subtleties she brought to her art. I will honor her as one of my true teachers until the day I die. However, from what you have just read, I am sure that you have already surmised Hollis's and my catering arrangement was destined to end in a bad way. If so, you were right.

It happened when we were in the woods, at a large private estate north of Chicago. There were three houses on the property, with appetizers offered at one house, the main course set out for a different house, and dessert for the third house. Hollis went into her usual tantrum and I finally lost my patience and stood up to her. She burst in to tears, responding, "No one has ever made me cry before." I assured her that was not my intention, that I was only trying to tell her that I would no longer listen to her rages. After that, she didn't want to have anything more to do with me. She quickly sought out other caterers to take my place. So we went our separate ways in 1997. I still see her around the city, about once a year, and she always says to me, "You are the best caterer in Chicago."

Hollis really stretched me, and for all that we did together, she, in the end, refused to help me when I applied to cater the prestigious Graham Room, which contracts to provide a three course French dinner to opera patrons in forty-five minutes, fully taking into consideration all dietary restrictions. It is the kind of event where you don't make any money, but where the prestige of catering to it is worth the loss. In fact, I catered Mrs. Graham's parties and she loved my food. She was from France and truly knew and enjoyed the many subtleties of culinary art. There are a lot of people who think they know, but they really don't.

Mrs. Graham knew. She is the most elegant lady in Chicago.

Hollis had successfully catered the Graham Room when she was with Chicago Caterers and she knew how to get it and to keep it. When I asked her for her help, she refused, saying, "You're not ready for it. I won't help you."

Now there is something in me that sort of snaps whenever I hear that. I say inside to myself, 'Oh, yes, you are ready. Yes, you can.' Then I do all I can to prove the person wrong. So I applied on my own, and had a great interview. In fact, they said that I gave the best answer anyone had ever given about the definition of service. But they ended up picking another company. I think they were reluctant to go with a really small caterer. As I reflect back on what Hollis said, I think she was right in one way. It wasn't that I wasn't ready. I know that I was. More to the point, it was that I didn't need it and that it wouldn't really help me.

Hollis's refusal to help me get the Graham Room contract, however, was the last straw regarding our professional relationship or anything that we might ever have done together after that. In my mind, I said, 'Thank you very much' and moved on. I had lost a chunk of business and we went our separate ways, but I still had enough gigs from other jobs to keep my business going. Those four years were very intense. I had the privilege of working for the most affluent leaders of Chicago society, and I knew that whatever we did, we needed to provide the expected five-star cuisine together with five-star service.

On the home front, Britha's asthma was getting worse and we were spending more and more time in hospital emergency rooms. After each of our daughters was born, I realized that they were the truly important ones in Edita's life. It hurt to know that, to feel it, and I didn't have the inner tools at that time to express my hurt. Consequently, I became an even greater workaholic *and* alcoholic. Whenever I looked within, I knew that I wasn't good enough, would never be good enough. I wasn't worthy. I didn't belong — as a husband, a dad, a business owner or respected caterer. If someone paid me a compliment, I would, in my own mind, find a dozen reasons why something could have been better. It didn't matter how many accolades were heaped on my head, I didn't believe any of them. After catering events, I would invariably take a huge glass of vodka from the party with me and go to a favorite bar and play pool and get really drunk. When I got really drunk, I didn't have to think about how I didn't belong, how unworthy I was.

As Edita took on the full-time job of researching alternative medical modalities that might help Britha to lead a normal life, I know she was also concerned about me and my drinking, especially since I began drinking more and more. In fact, one morning when I woke up on the living room sofa after getting totally blitzed, my entire family was seated around me, and thereafter began what in AA is called an intervention. Of course, I was not receptive to it. It took me a while to figure out what was going on, even though some of them were in tears as they spoke about their concern for me. I think I even asked if they all wanted to go to breakfast after they had spilled their hearts out. It must have seemed crass to them for me to even suggest it, but I suppose it was an accurate reflection of how deeply prepared I was to hear them, which was essentially, not at all, at least on the subject of my drinking. My healing would not come from my family, despite their love. It would come from outside the family circle.

My first healer was Dr. Tony Lu. My brother Norman, who now goes by Christian Cristiano, was working in Tony's office and spoke very highly of him. Tony at that time was in a shared alternative medicine practice, and he was an expert in acupuncture among other Chinese modalities of healing. Edita kept insisting that I get a complete physical, so I made an appointment with Tony, knowing that I would pass with flying colors. And I did.

I was very direct with Tony and told him about my addiction and my lifestyle and asked him if he could help me. He replied that he could and would, but that if I ever decided to change my lifestyle, that he would also be glad to help me with that, too. His acceptance of me, *just as I was*, was overwhelming, almost like Divine Love flowing from him through me. I wept tears of joy during that first acupuncture treatment, dozing off from time to time. After the treatment, I went to urinate before leaving the office, and was flabbergasted when all kinds of toxins, bubbling like a Frankenstein experiment, came out. It certainly helped me to embrace the many advantages of acupuncture. Tony's quiet and undemanding support and affirmation allowed me to begin dropping my defenses, although that process would take several years. Tony later went on to become the Director of the Alternative Medicine Program at Loyola University, and has recently taken a similar position for a hospital system in China.

I knew that my body was taking a terrible beating, not just from my excessive work schedule, but also from the ever increasing amounts of alcohol in my system. I also knew that I would need some help, and so

I sought out my friend Greg Victor, who is a colonics expert. He was very sensitive to my addiction, and he was the second of three healers who would prove instrumental in my survival. Greg Victor also did cranial sacral work. He was wonderfully calm and serene, in stark contrast to Edita, who was at her wits' end. Greg accepted me just for who I was, and didn't mandate that I change anything about myself or life. First with Tony, and then with Greg, I experienced, perhaps for the first time in my life, unconditional love.

It was thanks to Edita that I met Chuck Skelton, the third healer who has had such an enormous influence on transforming my life. Chuck has been many things in his life — a minister, a psychotherapist, a professor of ministry, and a counselor. Later in his career he chose to embrace his Native American roots, and became a traditionally trained healer of Blackfoot Indian descent. He is the founder of the Bear Spirit Medicine Lodge, a non-profit community based in Chicago through which traditional Blackfoot Ways are taught and community ceremonies are offered.

Chuck belonged to a group of alternative healers that took turns offering programs in their homes. On the day that he hosted the meeting, Edita wanted me to accompany her. I fought against her wishes, but I was still in the doghouse for having gone on a three day bender. When we arrived at Chuck's home, he immediately picked up how out of sorts I was and how much I didn't want to be there. He invited me to go to his office and when I walked in, I found myself surrounded by all kinds of healing tools — bones, feathers, claws, and animal skins. I felt the deep and sudden connection communicated to me by those healing agents and it was almost overwhelming. All I could do was look at Chuck and ask, "What do I do?"

The next weekend I attended a retreat with ten others, to begin learning about alternative healing as taught by the Blackfoot tradition.

69

During that weekend I somehow opened up a woman's star connection and Chuck, who was standing behind me, observed, "See. You belong." And I burst into tears and cried the whole weekend. I had been yearning and searching and wanting to belong my entire life, but never had managed to do so. Now I had been named as one who had the potential to become a healer. To know myself in this deeper way opened the door to seeing myself and my gifts in a larger context. Since then, I have studied with Chuck once a week for the better part of six years. Recently Chuck said it was okay that we now only need to meet every other week. Just as with Greg and Tony, it was Chuck's unconditional love for me that enabled me to begin to quiet and dissolve my inner defenses.

Then came the second AA challenge. Once again, I woke on my living room sofa to find family and friends waiting to tell me how much they loved me and how worried they were about my drinking patterns. This time I pushed back really hard. Everyone knows that alcoholism is a disease of denial; in fact, in my experience, I would call it the supreme disease of denial. I didn't suggest we all go to breakfast this time. I really wanted to throw them all out. Instead, I packed up and moved out myself, not wanting to hear any more of their litany.

But Edita was done. I had been disappearing for many nights, so she gave me notice. I called my oldest friend, Martin Escutia and asked if I could come over. I'm sure he expected that I was only coming for a night or two. When I arrived, and he saw me carrying a box up the stairs, he just shook his head. He didn't even help me carry any of my stuff up. When I started ragging on Edita, he held up his hand and said, "You will not do that here. Understand?" And I agreed and shut up.

Martin and I had first met when Terczak thrust me in as the cook at Gordon Restaurant during my externship from the Culinary Institute of America. Martin made sure that I wouldn't fail, taking a chance that

70

I would turn out to be a decent and reliable friend and fellow worker. He was one of the few cooks with whom I could disappear. We would be out of communication for years at a time, but then we would regroup.

As I look back, I see that my move to Martin's was my declaration to one and all that I would not give up my drinking. Yet those fourteen months when I crashed with Martin would prove to be my last year or so of partying. Tony Lu invited me to join a group of people going to China to study Xi Gong healing. We would visit and stay at Bejing's Xi Gong Institute, run by Master Wan, who is a Xi Gong master and also a medical doctor.

It was during my first trip to China, at the Xi Gong Institute, that I consciously connected the importance of food and healing to food and health. We had a guest speaker, an herb expert, who came in and very nonchalantly spoke about various kinds of herbs and foods and how they helped the body. The meals at the Institute were so simple and *so* good. That's when I really began to take notice and to admit to myself the power of food, specifically food that has been raised naturally with no additives, food that we call organic. But I couldn't really look at it then, because my whole business then was based on traditional, non-organic food. Yet I could also not remain unmindful of the obvious value of organic food and the benefits it had most probably given to Britha in her to return to full health.

My return trips to China and visits to Mongolia in subsequent years, under the leadership of Tony Lu, only served to confirm to me a growing conviction of the importance of organic food. To visit a country where there is very little processed food, and to taste the exquisite freshness and vitality of the vegetables and fruits, is its own confirmation of what we are missing if we continue down the road of processed foods. Some who were with me on those journeys reported that they ate more in China and Mongolia than they did in the United States, but actually *lost* weight. I felt that my consciousness was being raised, yet I would find that I still had some major lessons to learn.

The biggest lesson came when I was visiting my brother Christian in San Diego over the Christmas holiday in 2003. He wanted me to go with him and his friends to a Macy Gray concert at a nearby casino. It was a small venue, with about five hundred people, all standing around and drinking. I didn't really want to go, but they insisted. I hated walking by all those gray and greasy clones pulling on the slot machines. It gave me the creeps. When the band came out, led by Macy Gray, I knew immediately that she was both drunk and high and instantly, in a moment of unexpected epiphany, I saw myself in her and could tell how her band loathed and hated her, but they kept the music going. She would take twenty minute breaks and her band would keep playing, and each time she came back, wobbling even worse than before, even more smashed. For me, it was a most uncomfortable and unwanted identification, but every bit of it devastating and damning. It sucks when you're a user, because when you're a user, it's everybody else's fault and never yours, if you can admit you're a user.

And with so profound and accurate a mirror thrust in front of me, I realized with enormous pain how my staff at work and Edita at home had been keeping it all together for *me*, very much in the same way. I was disgusted with myself and wanted to throw up and leave, to escape, but I couldn't. Everyone else was having a ball. So I stayed and made myself watch. I called Edita early in the morning and said, "I'm coming home." And that was it, simple as that.

When I came home, I asked my mentors what I should do, and they recommended that I begin to go to hotroom yoga and to AA meetings and also to some therapy sessions with Edita. I set up a meditation room, which helped. I went public by announcing my alcoholism, and I got a lot of support from friends and family. For the first couple of months I was euphoric with my decision and the changes and healing that it was bringing into my life. Then the feelings of shame came crashing in, and that was a challenge. Fortunately, my mentors knew that this would happen, and they were prepared to be there for me when it did, and they were. I couldn't have gotten through it without them. I was deeply ashamed for the kind of husband, dad, and friend that I had been.

It can be difficult to forgive others who have wronged you or betrayed you, but it is even more difficult to forgive yourself. My trips to China and Mongolia and my work with Chuck Skelton stood out as foundations for what became an intense ongoing self-inquiry and its subsequent karmic healing, which in turn brought transforming moments that allowed me to finally forgive myself. My head was really deep in the sand for always getting yelled at by Edita. When I finally could be with my three mentors who accepted me and loved me without conditions, it allowed me to become vulnerable and honest enough to be able to see myself with greater clarity and self-love. When one can finally, truly forgive oneself, it releases all kinds of energies and potentials which can be directed toward healing, loving and serving others.

When I started going to AA, they said that I should find something to replace my drinking. Of course, I didn't believe them. After four months, I knew they were right. So I began to meditate every day, and gradually the germ of an idea for a new way of helping others unfolded in my mind, and found form in the Organic School Project. Many of the pieces came together quite quickly, but something was still missing, and it took me four or five months to finally recognize and welcome it. Regarding food, how it is produced and processed and distributed — that essential piece involved the utter importance of forgiving all the big companies for any past wrongs, by omission or commission. And it was my ability to forgive myself that had opened the door to forgive others, even those very individuals and companies that had played roles in bringing our current food system into existence. I realized that if I were going to serve as an instrument for clarity and positive change, that I would need to walk in forgiveness, honoring all, and I continue to do so.

Chapter Six
Walking in Forgiveness

BLOODLETTING WAS ONCE AN ACCEPTED PRACTICE for bringing balance and healing to the afflicted. Today it is almost inconceivable that its practice spanned nearly two millennium. Fortunately, in the last one hundred years, we have evolved in our knowledge of medicine and the human body, moving well beyond something that now seems both bizarre and barbaric.

Those who practiced bloodletting genuinely believed in its efficacy, intending only to bring restored health to those who had sought them out; however, had these practitioners known then what we know today, they would most certainly have abandoned their work. As flawed as their approach may seem, they were nevertheless doing their best.

No matter how imperfect their actions may appear, people are always doing their best. As Dr. David Hawkins has so often observed, if people could do better than they do, they would. Such a disarming insight offers a new lens, a new context, through which to view human striving and growth. It also allows us to embrace a deeper compassion for others and to walk in forgiveness, that is, *if* we choose to do so. And *if* we choose to forgive, we come to discover that we also end up forgiving ourselves, as well.

Little good, if any, comes from raging against what is past. Yet forgiveness need never condone what has been done, either by design, neglect, or out of sheer ignorance; instead, it can offer us a potential door through which a better, more responsible, and healthier way might be discovered. Increasingly today we find ourselves confronting problems that we have inherited from several centuries of poisoning our planet with reckless abandon, as well as the ongoing pillaging of vital resources that works against their natural restoration.

Today's soils are sick and depleted, having been for years poisoned by manmade chemicals in the form of fertilizers as well as by dangerous toxins found in the by-products of the Industrial Revolution, such as chlorine compounds, coal-tars, among others. Nobel laureate Dr. Alexis Carrell warned the world in 1912 of the urgent need to protect the quality of our world's soil in his book *Man, the Unknown*, suggesting that the health of living things, including humans, is directly related to the health and fertility of the soil, since all food comes from the soil. Carrell outlined how natural minerals in the soil create a harmony and balance that is disrupted by artificial fertilizers and chemical wastes.

According to Dr. Carrell, the chemicals in fertilizers seek union with the minerals already present in the soil, resulting in plants becoming unbalanced and unhealthy. Initially plants that are given artificial fertilizers look healthy and robust, but only because of an increase in their watery tissues, which reduces their protein constitution and makes them more prone to disease. As a result, the nutritive value of our food has greatly suffered and diminished in the past century. It is sadly ironic that even though crop yields have increased two or three fold as a result of artificial fertilizers, the quality and nutrition in the crops produced has been enormously reduced in favor of providing produce that looks better than it tastes. There are still those with us who were alive before World War II who remember how radically different, better and tastier food was prior to the decision that shelf-life was more important than nutrition and flavor.

In their astounding book, *Secrets of the Soil*, authors Tompkins and Bird report on the research findings of Dr. Joseph D. Weissman, a professor at the UCLA College of Medicine. After years of research, Dr. Weissman has concluded that most of the non-infectious diseases that debilitate humanity are of recent origin, their onslaught coincidental to the poisons produced by our ever-increasing industrial society and its inevitable toxic waste and, consequently, its universal pollution. Today toxins are everywhere on our planet: in our air, water, food, and soil. It is little wonder that the immune systems of so many have become so compromised. Part of this problem has been from the increasing use of chemical fertilizers for over one hundred and fifty years, which has imperiled the health of the soil in ways that most people don't realize.

A German chemist, Justus von Liebig, now called by many the "father of chemical agriculture," erroneously concluded in his experiments that plants are nurtured by nitrogen, phosphorous, and potash. Liebig's extensive writing and promulgation of this discovery led to the emergence of an industry that offered new synthetic chemicals that supposedly would enrich the soil. Prior to Liebig, common wisdom supported the theory that humus, the dark organic material in the soil that comes from the decomposition of vegetable and animal matter, played a central role in the soil's richness and fertility. Not realizing that his assumptions were mistaken, Liebig alleged otherwise, and his writings successfully bamboozled the world's farmers. According to Tompkins and Bird, Liebig finally discerned his initial error a decade later, but by then his discovery and advocacy had launched a great leviathan in the form of an ever-increasing and prosperous industry that manufactured and sold artificial chemicals that would ultimately weaken and imperil the natural richness of the soil used in growing crops.

After World War II, with a critical shortage of labor at home, farmers were desperate for any potential help that might assist them to increase their crop yields. The chemical companies, with the war no longer raging, were only too happy to oblige them by reinvesting their wartime profits into broad-spectrum pesticides, similar to DDT. Of course, these new chemicals continued poisoning the soil and killing the very microorganisms that create fertility. Sadly, the wide-ranging use of such fertilizers have also apparently caused an increase in degenerative diseases in humans, a poisoning that masqueraded as the modern and safe way to increase crop abundance, although there were a few sane and knowing voices that were courageously raising the alarm against its onslaught.

You may be asking, "Why should I forgive such horrible things that have been done and *that are being done* to our planet's soil, crops and people?"

REMEMBER: Forgiveness need not condone an act that is being forgiven; instead, think of it as a potential door through which new solutions and actions might be discovered. Wringing our hands or shouting down an alleged monster does very little good, either in the short run or the long run. Why should anyone who has the power and means to help make positive changes do so, especially under scathing attack?

REMEMBER: We are, all of us, responsible, either by omission or by commission. Not one of us is exempt. Furthermore, we do not know the what others' face. The quotation, commonly attributed to Philo of Alexandria, "Be kind, for everyone you meet is fighting a great battle" can help bring compassion for others as well as for ourselves.

So let's look at several of the presumable villains in this drama, to see if we might be able to better understand their various points of view. The first is the American farmer who, wanting to increase his hard-earned income and struggling to remain viable during the Great Depression, allowed himself to be enticed and encouraged by the chemical companies to lace his fields with all kinds of artificial fertilizers. Their promise to him of larger yields at first seemed true, to all appearances. But, as mentioned earlier, fertilizers seek union with the minerals already present in the soil and the plants, as a result, become unbalanced and unhealthy. At first the artificial fertilizers make plants look healthy and strong, but experience demonstrates that they are not what they appear to be and, in fact, are much more vulnerable to disease and pests. And even though crop yields have increased significantly, the quality and nutrition they offer has been enormously reduced in favor of providing a product that looks better than it tastes.

Thus the farmer, trusting the so-called experts and wanting to increase his income, shook hands with the devil of ignorance and implemented the recommended regimens of artificial fertilizers. Only after it was too late did he realize his error, for by then large corporate structures were rapidly replacing the once commonplace American family farm. Just as the farmer had too eagerly jumped for the promise of more profit, so, too, have the corporations made the moniker "big is better" a recurring theme in the do's an don'ts of modern farming and crop production. Perhaps "bigger is cheaper" was also an unstated, but understood, component of the rush to buy up small farms and to create megafarms, where as much as possible could become mechanized the better to save in labor costs and other attendant expenses.

Now, what is the necessary prime directive of any company? To make a profit, else the company will cease to exist. Company directors and administrators continually search, and sometimes scrounge, for ways to increase their profits and stock prices. That is to be expected, and any enterprising director or manager worth his salt would enthusiastically embrace such a notion. But then comes this question: exactly how far may individuals go to secure profit and advancement for the company to which they are responsible? Is there ever any justification for placing potential profits and company growth above and beyond the public good or the public safety? It would seem that such choices are rarely presented in black and white, but rather in subsequent striations of gray where there exist such things as contingency

79

management, percentages regarding acceptable levels of allergy, illness or even death, and perhaps some modicum of soul-searching. It would be giving short-shrift to corporate leaders to invoke the old saying, 'The higher you rise on the corporate ladder, the more they own of your soul.' It is much more likely that such decision makers genuinely believe in what they are doing and have become convinced that they are doing the right thing. Do such decision makers *actually realize* the horrendous, earth-destroying toxins that their companies' products are releasing into the soil in the name of fertilization and growth, or do they merely rely on the favorable studies and reports rendered by their scientists? Or do such decision makers seek refuge in that convenient kind of disconnect, a selective mental stance of 'not' knowing, perhaps hidden somewhere on an unconscious level where ethics and facts never meet?

Regrettably, there must also have been some scientists and managers who knew, and knew only too well, the far reaching and deleterious effects on the soil that accrue from the use of artificial fertilizers. Perhaps it was for 'the good of the company' or for the 'good of their bank accounts' that they chose short term gain over the on-going health of the Earth's soil. Greed has manifested its ubiquitous head in nearly every corporation and institution that has ever existed. The difference here is that this greed has befouled our planet's very life blood.

This great leviathan, born from the loins of Liebig's mistaken assumption, and was compounded by his promulgation of the same. It became so powerful so quickly that even Liebig didn't know how to stop it when he finally discovered his error ten years after his initial discovery. What price has the soil of our planet subsequently paid for the steady increase and application of artificial fertilizers and chemicals during these last one hundred and fifty years? The problem today, of course, is how to change the unthinkably destructive course that was set so long ago. Huge interconnected, multinational industries have become exceedingly successful at servicing the current systems of food production and distribution, a system which, when brought under keen scrutiny, raises troublesome questions and even graver concerns.

Yes. It is true that for many years, for whatever reason, a lot of people and many companies elected to drain resources and to make money. Is it any different than each of us deciding to use some left over pie dough to make a small pie, rather than throwing it out.

Some individuals no doubt truly thought what they were doing would help us grow more food and feed more people, perhaps never even considering the consequences of dumping lots of chemicals into our planet's soil. We now know that these chemicals, which have ended up in our water, our bodies, and our food kill the soil, the soil's helpers, and ultimately us! They also wreak havoc with our immune systems and make us more vulnerable to disease.

In retrospect, it is easy to point fingers of accusation at the big corporations, the research universities, the big ad companies and the government agencies. If we further extend that finger pointing, we will discover that those fingers are pointing at our ancestors as well as at us! The truth is that we have all had a part in destroying this planet, either by commission or omission. And we can't move on unless we forgive ... everyone, especially ourselves. An acceleration of the healing process will happen if everyone can take his or her own piece of responsibility. And please remember, forgiving does not mean that we like, condone or agree with something that some one or some company has done. But until we forgive, we will remain at a stalemate — it will be nothing more than a us/them, we/they standoff. That hasn't worked very well for anyone so far, has it? We're sick, and getting sicker. And so is the soil of our planet.

As I stated earlier in this chapter, I believe that any answer that has even the slightest chance of working must include forgiveness. In fact, forgiveness must be its enduring cornerstone, for ultimately the responsibility for the condition of our world comes back to each of us. If we cast honest eyes at our current situation, it won't take much to realize and to admit that we are all remiss, that we have all played a part in helping the world to become so fragile, so polluted — either by omission or commission. Whether through ignorance, neglect, disinterest, apathy or greed, or some other avenue, we are all responsible for the health of this planet that we share together.

One reason that forgiveness is our best first step toward a better, healthier world is that not one of us knows enough to lay blame and accusation on others. We cannot discern another's intent or the various pressures and motivations that resulted in what seem now to have been misinformed or self-serving choices. No matter what party was involved and no matter what choice was made, all individuals were doing the best they could. When we can accept that everyone was or is doing his or her best, we can then forgive — fully acknowledging what has happened, carefully assessing our current need, and joining together to find productive solutions for our shared journey. Recriminations and blame will only alienate those whom we need most to step up to the plate to join us in looking for a better way.

How do I know, from the very depth of my being, that forgiveness is the answer, the fundamental way we must go? For the simple reason that such a need was manifested in my own life on New Year's Eve in 2004, as I recounted in Chapter Five of this memoir. The need for forgiveness, both of myself and for all others, will now be forever a part of my own life's journey.

It is not something that came easily. My honeymoon after I quit drinking lasted about sixty days, during which time I enjoyed a profound happiness and exquisite joy. I had been warned about an imminent crash by those at AA meetings and by Chuck Skelton. When it arrived, I found myself in torrents of shame about how I had lived my life. I saw clearly how I had been a not-always-present dad and husband and how I had blamed my ex-wife for everything. I saw how I blamed others at work for whatever pain I felt within myself.

I had to admit these things, first to myself and then to others. Gary Reynard's book *The Disappearance of the Universe*, especially its recommended affirmations for forgiveness, proved enormously helpful. It enabled me to forgive myself for how I had been a dad and husband and how I had been around alcohol. As I became involved in the Organic School Project, I began to realize the double standard I had been living: eating organic food at home but not using it in the workplace. I needed to forgive myself for having ignored what was being served to kids in schools. My oldest daughter, Asa, tried to tell me for years about the kind of food her peers were being given at school, but I conveniently chose to ignore her. When I realized that I had become part of the problem by ignoring it, I began to ask forgiveness for having done so.

When I began to promote the concept of the Organic School Project, Gary Reynard's book helped me to get through a lot of tough meetings with the Chicago Public School District. Had it not been for that book, I would have been triggered a number of times and probably lost any credibility. Self-pity and anger merely plug us up. And, in a way, it's easier to extend the gift of forgiveness in that kind of setting, as opposed to one's own family. The closer we are to people, the harder it is to work through what needs to be addressed. At least, that's been my experience.

Nevertheless, it is not easy to wake others to the problems inherent in having a compromised food system. These mega corporations have been on a feed-Wall-Street kick forever, with their slick "Grow Growth Now!" slogans. And in the name of short term profit, we poison the earth, destroying its soil, resulting in an enormous ripple effect. Hence, we find ourselves walking on ill soil, drinking ill water, and eating ill food. We continue to slowly kill ourselves, our children and our planet. And owing to *how* animals are slaughtered and produce is grown, with one person tending one thousand acres of harvest, we are unwittingly eating angry and sad food.

The 8,000 square mile dead zone in the Gulf of Mexico is a direct result of our using chemicals to grow our cotton, wheat and beans. Boats, working 24/7, dredge 462 tons of silt at the mouth of the Mississippi every day, which is then taken and deposited in a deeper part of the Gulf of Mexico. That silt is full of chemicals that release nitrogen, and when that silt sinks to the bottom of the Gulf, it sucks up all the oxygen, killing all of the tiny organisms that feed the fish. At last count, there were more than 165 such dead zones around the planet. Why is such activity allowed to continue? Perhaps in the name of profit. Perhaps in the name of it simply having become the commonly acceptable thing to do.

Did you know that here in Illinois, which boasts some of the richest tillable soils in the world, ninety-five percent of our food is imported from outside the state? Instead, Illinois soils are devoted to growing corn and beans. Did you know that school lunch program foods are comprised mostly of corn-based products? The United States now imports more than half of its food. In grocery stores, we mistakenly think that the some 45,000 items being offered reflect abundance, but that is totally wrong. A vast majority of products in our food system are imbued with chemicals that wreak havoc with our immune systems and offer no real nutrition. It's little wonder that most people are on some kind of medicine as well as feeling depressed and disconnected.

Did you know that Mexico's once indigenous corn is gone? Twenty years ago there were over one hundred varieties that had existed there for centuries. What is happening has worldwide ramifications, because everyone and everything is dynamically interconnected. Would you believe that we now have only five seed companies left in this world? Companies were allowed to patent seeds beginning in 1982. Believe it or not, there is also a current movement to genetically engineer food produce in ways that it will also serve as "medicine" that will be prescribed by your primary physician.

Did you know that we currently use 2.4 percent of the world's tillable land to grow the cotton that we produce? Yet we also use a staggering 25% of the annual consumption of pesticides to grow that cotton! Look in your bedroom closet. Are all of your clothes manufactured through an organic process? If not, you (and I) remain part of the larger problem. I dearly wish that I could afford an entire wardrobe of clothes that have all been organically produced, but I can't, and so I contribute to the further poisoning of our planet.

It will be important for forgiveness to occur at all levels, such as with the big corporations and the government agencies that have not served us as well as we might have hoped. And they're not stupid. At least *some* of their executives fully realize the mess they've gotten us into. I'd like to shout this question to them, "So how's that working out for you?" We all know, or we are coming to realize, that it's not working out very well at all, for *any* of us. Yet all of that notwithstanding, I adamantly believe that any and all forgiveness is going to have to begin with one's self, if we are ever going to successfully join together to solve the many problems that are staring us in the face. That is why I believe that forgiveness is necessary. In my experience, it is the first best step toward the most expeditious way of getting beyond the blame game. It frees us to join together so that real and enduring solutions can be found for our current difficulties. Is any larger purpose served in hanging on to the past and recriminating others, while the very future and health of our planet now needs us and is calling to us to chart a new, healthier course?

An important part of the changes that are emerging will involve all of us steadfastly voting with our dollars. Real and lasting change will only come when homemakers insist on organic food and apply verbal pressure to their local grocery stores and restaurants. Don't give them any of your money unless they are willing to accommodate your request to change and to do the right and healthy thing. And take care to know what's going on. Currently there are three categories for organic food: 75%, 85% and 100%. Remember: a product that is 95% organic might still contain five percent of undesired chemicals. We don't need new policies, for it was the government and big companies got us into this mess to begin with. What we need is to vote with our dollars, and we can do it, especially if enough people join together to do so. The big companies are built on making profit, and if they begin to see that their potential profits are in danger of eroding, they will take measures to accede to public demand.

Each of us can only do so much. Chapter Eight will offer suggestions for how each of us, even in small ways, can begin to make positive differences toward the sustainability of our planet and its resources. The important thing is to begin doing something positive to help our world, even in a small way. Owing to my background and training, one of my own personal goals is to assist schools in going completely organic in the food that they offer to their students as well as to encourage students to grow and harvest some of that food. The next chapter outlines, from our experience, some why's, how's, do's and don'ts — hard lessons that were derived from our pilot program within three Chicago elementary schools. My hope is that what we learned will prove beneficial and will help others who may join us in our continuing effort to afford to our nation's school children food that is nutritious, tasty and safe.

My larger goal, and I know that it will only be achieved if there is a large outpouring of public demand and support for it, is for our entire nation ultimately to return to local food systems, food systems that are entirely organically-based and self-supporting. Here is a sobering example of what we are doing to ourselves. A friend of mine who lives in Sedona recently reported to me that she had placed an apple that she had bought at a local market out into her garden for any birds or animals that might want it. The apple sat there, day after day, until it rotted. It caused her to wonder about the apple and why it wasn't even touched. A few days later she bought an organically-produced apple and put it in the same spot, and it was eaten within twenty-four hours. Our planet's animals appear to be a lot wiser than we are about what they allow themselves to ingest.

When one remembers that a small example like this is reflective of a much larger system and its perils and failures, it is staggering to ponder the vastness of these current challenges. In truth, there is very little that most of us can do to change the world for the better. Nevertheless, within such individual change comes hope for the preservation of our species and planet, I am reminded of what Leo Tolstoy once wrote: "Everyone thinks of changing the world, but no one thinks of changing himself." Ultimately, I can only change myself and, with that, hope that my subsequent choices and actions will make a positive difference.

Chapter Seven
Lessons Learned, The Organic Food Project

ONE OF LIFE'S ENDURING TEACHERS IS EXPERIENCE, and who among us does not now wish that more had been known about a particular endeavor before a commitment, albeit with all good intentions and unbridled enthusiasm, was made?

In retrospect, our initial attempt to establish a viable and continuing organic food emphasis in public school cafeterias through the establishment of the Organic School Project failed because of the lack of what Peter Senge calls SHARED VISION. For any program to survive *and* thrive, there must be a "buy in" among supporters on all levels of an organization. Otherwise, the program remains as fragile as a flower, and the loss of one key supporter can bring its termination. In the case of our Organic School Project, it was the retirement of the director of food services for the Chicago Public School system. That event taught us an enduring lesson of the essential need for shared vision at all levels.

The idea for the Organic Food Project came to me gradually, through almost a half a year of reflection and meditation. However, I also knew for the longest time that some key piece was missing, and I kept searching for it. When I first started to attend meetings of Alcoholics Anonymous after my return to Chicago from San Diego, I was told that I would need something bigger than myself to replace my former occupation of drinking. Of course, I thought that I knew better. But after six months of watching television and eating butter pecan ice cream each night of my life, I knew that the advice that had been given to me was right on. So I started to ask myself in my meditations how I could give back to my community and world, and the concept of an Organic School Project gradually emerged. The image of feeding kids more positive foods™ became ever increasingly clear, as did the realization that kids are disconnected with Mother Earth, necessitating that a vegetable garden be established for each school, so that kids could reconnect with the soil and where food comes from.

That next December, my brother Christian (whom my parents had named Norman), called me and wanted me to come visit him so that we could both go and hear a guru from India named Siva Baba. I had been sober for a year and was really busy and didn't want to go. But Christian persisted, and I finally told him to go ahead and book me a flight and place. For me, it was going to be just another trip.

When I got there, Christian and I went directly to the program. Siva Baba's assistant, Vagee, came out on the stage and was, to my eyes, a beaming and pure white light like something I had never before seen. She talked to us for a while, and then Baba came out. He just stood there for at least ten minutes, slowly looking at each one of us. Then he started to talk with us, and his guided meditations were extremely powerful. I had never experience that state of consciousness before, and it reminded me of my old days at *est*, when I really went deep.

On day two, my third eye opened during one of the meditations. It was when Baba invited us to imagine the sun and the moon, each eating the other and traveling in an elliptical circle, in sort of an oval trajectory. And I whispered to Christian, "My God! You are *not* going to believe this!"

Later during that seminar, I bought a CD Baba had made that specifically focused on removing negative karma and I listened to it every day for four months. Then I went on line and bought all of his CDs and signed up for every available workshop. Then they put out a request that said that if anyone wanted to study with Baba one on one that they would accept up to five. I applied and got in. Thereafter I would travel to India to visit and learn all that I could. It grew into a beautiful friendship, for which I will be forever grateful.

Early on I realized how much I had to learn about meditation and I began to meditate more and more. On my trips to India, I learned how to go even deeper into meditation. Baba also let me teach some classes. My medicine man mentor Chuck helped me to devise these classes, which dealt with identifying one's gifts, the need for forgiveness, and boundaries. It was very unusual for Baba to permit another teacher and also for him not to insist that I give up all teachers except him. He also let me keep up my work with Chuck.

Baba could do some amazing things, such as manifest *vibhuti*, which is a sacred ash used in Hindu worship and believed able to bring miraculous healing as well as to negate negative karma. He could also beam light from his eyes and there would only be white light where his eyes had been. Perhaps the most amazing phenomenon that I experienced was when I was attending one of his seminars at the Garrison Institute in Upstate New York, and during a meditation the brick walls of that old Capuchin monastery just melted away. They slowly disappeared, and I found myself sitting outside. It was as if we were all suddenly sitting outside of the building.

My two and a half years of study with Siva Baba were illuminating in many ways. He was the first person who helped me to understand what it means to "surrender" — just as he taught me how to subdue my logical mind in a way that encouraged accepting and allowing. It became apparent to me that the healing of a system requires surrendering it to God, whether it is a human body, a way of doing things, or even an Organic School Project. Baba taught me a lot about utter positivity and karma.

According to Baba, before coming into incarnation we all agree to take on various kinds of karmic debts and to pay them down. Imagine three file cabinets full of karmic debt. The first, the largest, is for our own past lives, and we take the largest portion from that; the next, which is smaller, is for our ancestral family, and we take some more from that; the last, the smallest, is for the collective world karma of humanity, and we take our share from that. We all take on negative karma from these cabinets before coming in, the better to learn new life lessons and also to atone for past mistakes and actions. I learned that my marriage and my frequent money struggles were of karmic origin, and that I was doing my best in this lifetime to bring balance to past imbalances.

Baba also taught me that actions, words and thoughts are all of equal power and importance. Our life and work here on Earth involves welcoming everything, walking in compassion and forgiveness in our thoughts, words and actions. If, instead, we feed our egos, we invite a lot of negative karma. If people only could understand how perfectly the system of karma works, they would realize that there can be no real self pity, because we each choose by our actions, words, and thoughts what happens to us. To be sure, we are sometimes still paying back on mistakes from other lifetimes, but the important thing is that we continue to learn and to evolve in our spiritual awareness.

As I came closer to Siva Baba's inner circle, I gradually began to see things about his organization that I thought he needed to hear. It is so easy for any inner circle to become stagnant and closed. I believe that Baba needed a second circle, an intersecting circle, with people who looked out, to balance the inner circle that tended to look "in" to him. Too often devotees place too much responsibility on a guru, expecting that guru to have all the answers. No one has all the answers; I had learned that during my days at *est* and at that Grateful Dead concert. Baba patiently listened to me as I told him what I thought he needed to know, after which time I thanked him and proceeded to terminate my studies. In retrospect, I would never trade those thirty months for anything. Siva Baba's teaching and presence had transformed me in a way that nothing else could, and I will always be grateful to him. In fact, it was my business plan for the Organic School Project that brought my acceptance into the one on one relationship. When he met with me after having received it, he lifted it up and said, "This is why you are on the planet." And I knew he was right.

To be sure, I had enjoyed my years of chasing pleasure, money, booze and fame — all of it to make me feel good. But I had gradually learned from Baba and Chuck and Tony that it wasn't all about me. Baba had always talked about selfless service. He said that one needs two things to be happy. The first is some sort of daily practice, meditation, prayer, or something like that. The other is selfless service. And when I began to consider what selfless service I could offer, questions kept coming to me about how it might be possible to add value to the current way we live and work with food and improve the way kids eat. I mean, what else could I do, with my background and training? It was a natural and it felt good and Baba had confirmed that it was part of my life's journey to do so.

As I opened myself to understanding how I might contribute to improving the way kids eat, my oldest daughter's many-a-year complaints about the food served in school finally began to sink in. Aja had been telling me forever how much her friends hated the food that was dished out to them at school. A large part of my inner discovery and transition was becoming ever increasingly aware of what is really going on and how it affects our kids. Most people don't have a clue, and if they did, they'd be appalled.

I realized that I just couldn't be an advocate for my kids, who were already taking organic lunches in to school for themselves, but rather an advocate for *all* kids. It needed to be about all the kids. The wealthy parents can afford to feed their kids organic food, and aren't usually aware of the impact that processed foods have on the other kids, and so they just along with it.

Out of meditation came a sense of mission and commitment to improving the food kids eat. Teaching about it came a little later, and then honoring and blessing the current food system, which was and is one of the hardest things to do, because it's not the system we want or need and it is certainly not a system that honors the planet. We are full of chemicals and poisons that have filled our environment, and most people don't even realize it. Dr. Harry Oldfield is a scientist from England who has adapted and perfected the use of Kirlian photography in his research since the early 1970s. His instruments capture the light energy that emanates from all living things. Dr. Oldfield gave the Keynote Address at the 2006 gathering of members of the International Society for the Study of Subtle Energies and Energy Medicine, and stated the following about some of his research: "We looked for the energy in two types of breakfast foods: muesli/granola and a type of popular cereal. We could not find any evidence of energy in the cereal. The weight of the samples were the same, but we looked and looked for the sunshine. We couldn't find it in any of our hundreds and hundreds of pictures. We [also] looked at the energy field of some organic oranges. The oranges showed evidence of a beautiful energy emanating from them."

Is that a wake up call? If it isn't, it should be. How many ways can one find to warn people that a lot of the food they eat is "dead" — has no energy, no nutrients, all in the name of shelf-life and profit.
Sometimes I feel like Henry David Thoreau after he was jailed for refusing to pay his taxes, because it supported our war with Mexico. Thoreau was looking out of his jail cell window and his mentor Ralph Waldo Emerson walked by and, upon seeing him, called out, "Henry.

What are you doing in there?" And Thoreau called back, "Ralph, what are *you* doing *out* there?" Our modern prisons are made of bricks of ignorance and apathy. And there is no more precious thing in this world than our children. If parents fully realized what they are condoning and consigning their children to eat at school, they would soon be demanding organic food for all kids. And why stop with kids, why not for all of us — everywhere? Of course such a radically and wonderfully healthy change in how we grow and transport food would require our returning to a regional food system, with regional suppliers, much as we once enjoyed in this country forty and fifty years ago and before that, when food itself tasted better because it *was* better. But how does one change an entrenched system? I knew that such change couldn't be forced upon the big players, and I suspected that any change that might happen would probably begin with our kids. So I kept asking myself what key component was missing in my emerging program to assist schools in serving better food.

As I meditated to discover how to best define the Organic School Project, I realized that some component was missing. It was like when you leave the house, and realize that you have forgotten something. Finally, after many months, the room suddenly got very bright and I realized what had been missing: Honor All. Honor Everything. It was only then that I could arrange for the final business plan to be written.

In order to move to a better place, it had become clear to me that all components of the larger whole needed to be honored, including the big food companies, the global food system, the school districts, the cafeteria workers, and so on. Rather than emphasizing what is wrong today and vituperating against past wrongs and current errors, it is essential that we forgive and move on ... TOGETHER. And if we are honest and remember that we all, either by commission or omission, have contributed to the current state of this enormous problem, it is

94

easier to forgive others as well as ourselves and to resolve to do, in whatever way possible, *something* that will make an enduring difference.

That is what the Organic School Project is all about: it's my way of giving back to others and of doing my best to ensure that students benefit from more positive foods. The central mission of the Organic School Project is to transform Chicago-area children into healthier, more mindful eaters, one school and one child at a time.

Some may wonder why there is a need for More Positive Foods™ in our schools. When compared with healthy children, obese children are four times more likely to experience some impairment in functioning at school. Such children miss an average of four school days a month. In addition, obesity almost doubles a child's risk for asthma. Obesity is also suspected to be an accelerating factor for the development of *both* Type 1 and Type 2 diabetes. Children in Chicago are two-and-a-half times more likely to be overweight than their peers nationwide. In some Chicago neighborhoods, the incidence of obesity in children between the ages two and twelve is as high as forty-seven to fifty-three percent. It is no exaggeration to warn that the health of our children is at stake, as did Dr. Julie Gerberding, Director of the Centers for Disease Control and Prevention, suggesting that our nation's number one health problem is "the epidemic of obesity that we are watching unfold before our very eyes." [From a Commencement Address, 2003]

The Organic School Project model is based on three essential components: Grow, Teach and Feed. Children are reconnected with their food sources through the establishment of school and community gardens. Students are also taught about the importance of nutrition, mindfulness and environmental stewardship through an integrated wellness curriculum. Finally, OSP provides More Positive Foods™ made from scratch through a school's food service, using organic and natural ingredients that are procured locally when seasonally available.

I developed the term More Positive Foods™ because I believed that we needed a way to describe foods that are "whole foods" — that is, foods without additives, preservatives, hormones, pesticides and other chemicals that are, ideally, made from human hands rather than processed by huge machines. I also realized that using the word "healthy" to describe the food I was advocating would be insulting to the large companies and corporations that provide such services, because the foods that they serve to students are "healthy" according to USDA standards, which among other things require minimum levels of certain vitamins and proteins. The large providers meet these require-ments by "fortifying" the food. That is a code word for pumping in artificial supplements, rather than natural ingredients. Over five billion free and reduced meals are served each year by the Federal Lunch Program. That is an amazing feat when you consider it! My goal is to develop a proven model that can be advocated and implemented into the larger system, thus adding value to what is already now in place. This urgently needed transformation must happen *within* the current system, rather than from blindly attacking it. That, of course, means that more money must be given to the system.

Three Chicago public elementary schools were selected and approved for our pilot program. Alcott School, with 489 students, included the following demographics: 36.4% African-American, 33.2% white, and 21.4% Hispanic, with 51.1% at the Low Income level. McCorkle School, with 300 students, had a 100% African-American population, with a 93.5% Low Income level. Hammond School, with 534 students, was represented by a 94.1% Hispanic population, 5.3% African-American, and .7% white student population, with an 89% Low Income level.

We had raised enough money to begin our program at Alcott School for 42 days, and we had more than our share of challenges. First, we had to follow all of the rules, including Federal Lunch rules, the Chicago Public Schools' rules, and the Chartwell-Thompson Compass Group rules.

The most difficult task was to fulfill the required nutritional levels, as mandated by the Federal Lunch Program. As mentioned earlier, the major providers manage to do this by adding synthetic ingredients and chemicals. Josephine Lauer-Washuk, my assistant, worked steadfastly at this task for more than a month, and we finally did it! It was ironic, though. From the beginning, we were using the very best ingredients that money could buy, and we were still under the minimum guidelines. We made lots of molasses/raisin cookies. You may be surprised to learn that the nutritional standards have not been changed since 1986. More worrisome is that the federal guidelines do not distinguish between the number of calories served to first graders as opposed to eighth graders. All students must receive the mandated minimum number of calories, and we wonder why grade school kids are becoming so chubby. Everyone notices this glaring discrepancy and imbalance, but the stock answer is always that 'we're just following the law.' You may be wondering how our More Positive Foods differ from current lunch-room offerings:

Greater than 70% of ingredients will be Organic from USDA Certified Organic Producers and Farmers.

Ingredients will be hormone-free, non-GE/GMO with limited exposure to pesticides, additives, preservatives and stabilizers.

All vegetables, starches, sandwiches, salads and other sides will be produced from scratch, on-site by the lunchroom staff; protein-based entrees will be made by an off-site UDSA-approved commissary kitchen and re-heated on site.

Vegetables will be fresh and 100% organic; frozen will only be used when fresh is not available; no canned vegetables will be allowed. When seasonally possible, fruits will be locally grown (within a 50 mile radius); no canned fruits will be served.

Whole grains will be present in all bread, cereal and tortilla products.

Seafood will be raised and harvested using sustainable methods, and tuna from dolphin-safe waters without unnecessary additives or preservatives.

Beef will be, at a minimum, hormone and antibiotic-free.

Poultry will be free-range and cage-free at a minimum.

Foods from the school gardens will be incorporated whenever possible.

You are also now probably wondering how you can enroll as a student in any of the schools that have adopted this program. And I am sure that you would agree that our children are our future, and that the more we can help to equip them to excel, the better it will be for all of us, including our nation's future. Part of how that can be done is to convince those who have the authority and power of the need to incorporate the Organic School Project model into the Federal School Lunch program mandates. As mentioned before, such a move would require a greater investment into the system, but it would be a sound investment in our nation's future, with the benefits to be observed over a lifetime of change.

Today schools receive about $ 2.42 to make a hot lunch. The Chicago School District takes out $ 1.50 of that to pay for staff and overhead. The food provider (Chartwell-Thompson) is left with $ .92, from which they subtract $ .40 for their disposables and overhead. Our cost per meal for the OSP was $ 2.52, thus requiring that we raise another $ 2.00 per meal, since Chartwell-Thompson was only going to give us $ .52. The additional cost charges, for three months, came to over $ 160,000, and was covered by the Organic School Project, thanks to our many supporters, including companies and individuals. The Chicago Public Schools spend more than $ 200 million annually on its food service program.

Others who have advocated the implementation of healthier quality foods in schools have failed because they attempted to force a gourmet cuisine on grade school kids and teenagers. We decided that we would start with the same menu as before, except that everything would be organic. On the first day, we made turkey tetrazzini with organic, frozen peas. The kids couldn't get over that the peas were green. We had to explain that peas are supposed to be green. We discovered later on that many of the kids didn't know that fresh fruit is supposed to be crunchy.

Students in Kindergarten through the fifth grade liked the organic food immediately. It took longer for the older kids to appreciate what we were doing, and initially they pushed back really hard. Of course, part of the reason is that their tastebuds are shot and they are totally addicted to the junk food they inhale. We did our best to explain the differences, and they began to buy in — but it was slow going at first. Perhaps one of our greatest triumphs was running out of ratatouille — the kids ended up loving it. We were showing them a different way and, in a way, we were raising their consciousness about their food, the world, and themselves.

Early in the program an eighth grader came up to me and said, "This food sucks." It hurt to hear that, but I knew she wasn't really talking about the food. She was really projecting and saying, "I suck." Many teachers came on board and before long the entire school, all three floors, was full of art work, all related to our project. It was so thrilling to see the coolers full of organic food. And the longer we served it, the more the kids settled down and ate stuff like vegetables and ratatouille. The lunch count went up eight percent in ten weeks. We also had gardens and garden volunteers at all of the schools. It was thrilling to watch kids witness how a tomato actually becomes a tomato. So many of them are disconnected from Mother Earth.

We also invited and encouraged interaction with Dietetic Interns from Loyola University Chicago's School of Nursing. They came and presented students and teachers with a year-long healthy eating curriculum.

99

Mindfulness is the moment-by-moment attention or awareness given to an activity (walking, eating), or to the self (breathing, muscle tensing), and is generally done with a non-judgmental mindset. A guided exercise in mindfulness can open up, expand and enhance a simple experience, such as eating an orange. We were most fortunate to have Dr. Chuck Dumont, the Director of Pediatric Nutrition and Director of the Pediatric Integrative Medicine Program at Loyola University Medical Center, oversee and supervise the delivery of mindfulness training in the classrooms for our project.

As I noted at the beginning of this chapter, our initial pilot program lost its key support when the director of food services for the Chicago Public Schools retired and her replacement refused to endorse what we were doing, saying, "I can only operate with money that I have in the bank. I can't operate on miracles." And when they pulled the plug on Hammond and McCorkle, I recommended to my board that we also pull out of Alcott in Lincoln Park. Is it right to do something like this for only prosperous schools? My board concurred unanimously. All kids in all schools deserve the most nutritious and best food we can supply to them. For many, it is their only real meal of the day. So one of our most important lessons is that a shared vision with multiple stakeholders is essential for the continuance of any program. If that is lacking, you are riding on the whim of fate.

Another second lesson was that honoring and blessing the system really works and has to continue. We need to walk in forgiveness and get beyond accusation and guilt-tripping for the sake of changing and improving the food we are offering to kids in their schools. As I have said many times, real change is going to come through the major players, and one goal for the Organic School Project was to provide and validate a model that actually works and that could be incorporated into the current system, albeit if larger resources could be found to sustain the extra costs.

The third lesson was what I had intuited about kids' tastes, that you really have to ease kids into more positive foods. Start where they are.

Begin with what they are accustomed to eating. Gradually, most of them will come around. And how we feed kids can't be holistic enough. If we can embark on such changes, the benefits will gradually be seen over the lifetimes of the students themselves.

Part of what I learned personally from our pilot study was patience. There is often a delay, especially with new programs. I am learning how to be comfortable with things not happening in the way that I expect, or in a time frame that I assumed.

With our original pilot program, it was an all or nothing arrangement with those who expressed interest in signing on. We now realize that such a condition is very limiting, and we are going to tailor our various program components in ways that will best help each specific school. We now have over forty schools that have requested our help or that have expressed interest in what we are doing. We are also developing curricula related to teaching things like gardening and wise eating choices.

I am also learning to surrender to whatever happens. I can now say to anyone interested in what we are doing, "If you're in, you're in; if you're not, you're not. And it's okay either way." And really mean it. I no longer feel the need to proselytize and to badger people on why they should be on this particular path. And I think a main reason for that is that we have in the pilot study a dynamic and proven program that speaks for itself, both in its results as well as in the anecdotal affirmations found in the stories of many who participated. There is nothing more compelling than that sort of "eye witness" testimonial, especially when it reports real transformations.

There were also personal transformations during the creation of the Organic School Project and I need to report those, if this memoir is to be fully honest and complete. The first was when I finally walked into my catering company's kitchen about three and a half years ago and announced to my chef Carlos that we were going to begin to go completely organic. The hypocrisy of eating all organic at home but not serving it to my customers finally caught up with me. Carlos pointed out that switching to antibiotic-free chicken would cost forty percent more than what we are then paying, which would be about another dollar a pound. We always used a lot of chicken breast. He asked how we could still do that and make money, and I said that I didn't know, but that we would do our best to figure it out as we went along. He asked, "Shouldn't we figure it out before we start?" I said, "No. We're going to start first, and *then* we'll figure it out. We're going to *force* ourselves to figure it out."

That was the beginning. I put my foot down and said we were going to go all organic, but then I realized that I didn't know how we were going to find the local organic suppliers. Whole Foods knows where they are, but they aren't going to tell you. I called around to all the fancy chefs who knew, but no one would tell me. It was not a surprise, however, and it brought back a disheartening memory of a meeting of over two hundred Chicago area chefs that happened about six months before I made my decision to go organic. The meeting was supposed to be all about going organic and I attended the gathering and asked about where one could get the local, organic food. In response, one of the two presenters answered a different question while the other glared at me as if I had betrayed him. These chefs were both on the cutting edge of the organic movement, but they were unwilling to share their experiences, including the successes and mistakes. This is a curious world, isn't it? All in all, I finally realized that I was on my own, and that I would have to figure it all out.

In way of doing just that, I asked a local organic food advocate, Tara Brockman, to take me to her father's farm. Henry Brockman has a nine acre vegetable farm, and I'll never forget my first visit. Tara and I parked on a muddy road and walked through a small wooded area to the top of a hill and beyond a clearing that revealed a small valley, which was Henry's nine acre patch of heavenly vegetables. The light was coming off the land as I walked down into the field, and I felt an enormous surge of energy, almost like love, emanating from the vegetables. It blew me away. I suddenly found myself down on the ground picking vegetables. Henry walked over to me and asked, "Who are you and what are you doing?"

Then he must have realized that nobody was home, because I was so totally engrossed in what I was doing. I vaguely remember mumbling something to him about needing a pan with hot oil so that I could make lunch for us. He just shook his head and walked away. After picking some vegetables, I made stir fry and several of us devoured it, and it tastes were transforming! I asked Henry to explain to me what he did and why he did it and who was growing the organic stuff, and he just started talking and that was when my awakening began. I visited two other farms that day, as well. Tara helps new farmers get started and she certainly helped me raise my consciousness that day. Before that, I had compartmentalized "organic food" into something we bought for Britha and our family at Whole Foods. Visiting the farm made the phenomenon or organic food real, and I began to instruct my staff to track all of the food we were buying at my company, because I had become curious about where it came from. I knew it wasn't organic, and I knew most of it didn't come from Illinois. My catering company had a chocolate chip cookie that was touted as the best of its kind in Chicago. That famous little cookie had 12,200 miles on it, for all of its ingredients. A turkey sandwich together with a pasta salad and a chocolate chip cookie turned out to have over 32,000 miles on it. And I began to see that it isn't truthful or responsible to eat like that, and I proceeded to visit hundreds of farms over the next three years. I knew that I needed to go direct and build my own distribution networks.

Having kept an exact weekly inventory at my catering company, I knew approximately what I would be needing each week. That enabled me to visit farmers to see if they had the produce I wanted, if a fair price could be agreed upon. A lot of what I needed was not available through the traditional food distribution system, which essentially required me to set up separate smaller systems of delivery for the items I bought. Sometimes it took up to four months to figure out how we could arrange to get the stuff. For example, I would search for empty refrigerator trucks returning to Chicago that might be willing to stop and get something for me and deliver it. In the industry, these are called "refer" trucks. One disappointment was that my fish guy and meat guy didn't want to play, and they used lack of insurance as an excuse for not helping. They'd rather come back to Chicago with an empty truck, than rock the boat or challenge the prevailing system. But that didn't stop us. It hurt for a minute, but we kept moving. Sabrina figured it all out. She was amazing. We worked well together. We found a distributor of high-end cheeses who came back to Chicago three times a week with empty trucks, and we were able to cut a deal with him. It comes down to "if there's a will [I want this item on my menu], then there's a way."

Once one goes local and organic, one becomes aware of and reliant on seasonal offerings. As I said earlier, that is how it all worked until about forty or fifty years ago. Today we can get asparagus all year, but in Chicago local asparagus is only available for about three weeks a year. The limitations are tricky at first, because people have come to expect anything they want any time they want it. My staff did a lot of teaching and talking, as did I . It was really a process of educating people. I didn't do it based on the quality of our food or chasing flavor. Instead I would talk about the environment in a positive way. For example, in Alaska and Washington State in March the salmon run, and it is the very best time to harvest them and serve them. If people wanted asparagus in January, I would tell them about my mushroom guy who has been raising mushrooms for over thirty years. His father had done it and he had gotten fascinated by it, too. I would also tell them about the antibiotic-free chicken that I would get from Ohio, and how wonderful it tasted. There is nothing like winter spinach and root vegetables. Eventually you find that you're not selling the food, but rather a story, a story that makes sense ecologically and honors the planet.

The kitchen staff all bought in immediately. They loved going to farmers' markets. Mostly Hispanic, they are more connected to Mother Earth and they know how to honor it. My sales staff were the hardest sells, and I knew that I couldn't just turn a key and bingo, they'd be on board. We needed to allow for their growing awareness. It's a process. That's where the dance comes in. It brings balance.

Our goal was, with every dish we served, to help the community and the environment, and we managed to make it half way to our goal after three years. Business went up by forty-two percent for sales volume during my catering company's last two years. We had earned the enviable reputation of having the best food and service in Chicago. I never talked about food and beverage and service with potential customers. Everyone is doing the same thing, and everyone is fighting on margin. People want that, and they're supposed to have it. They have a right to expect it. It's basic. But what we found was that deep down, people also wanted to feel that they were somehow contributing to the planet, somehow selflessly serving the greater good. Whenever we talked about this larger context, people really listened and were deeply touched. Most people want to contribute to the planet. It's the only planet we have.

I will never forget one catering event. I had to fly to Washington, D.C., to close the deal, and I told them what I planned to do. It involved my buying a cow and a half from an organic farm that was five or six hours from Chicago. I drove to the farm and stayed there a couple of days and met the cows' family. I put the prepared meat in my coolers and drove back to Chicago and served a party of 5,000 people, who couldn't stop talking about how I had honored the cow and respected Mother Earth. What most people don't know today is that they are eating angry, sad meat that has been treated disrespectfully. I pray that our society will not ignore this much longer. The negative energy inherent in our food must take some toll on our bodies and emotions. The Kamba Lama of Mongolia, that country's head medical lama, loves meat, but he refused to eat the standard meat offerings during his recent visit to Chicago. His host would alert me, and I would take some organically-raised, free range meat and prepare it for him, and he would eat it with great delight. Our nation's meat products contains much anger and sadness owing to the way we grow and butcher these animals. It certainly is long past time for a wake up call!

Can you imagine what would happen if people started going to their grocery stores and demanding organic beef and hormone-free beef? Just everyday people. Not the rich who can afford it. It's easy to feel helpless, but any real and enduring difference begins with individuals and grows from there. The stores do listen when customers make requests. They want and need the business. So we need to be clearer with them as to what we'll buy and won't buy. Why should any of us buy food that is inherently bad for us, both for the chemicals and hormones that were pumped into it as well as for the way it was cultivated, harvested, and slaughtered? The answer is: We shouldn't! Let's face it. No one is going to force the big companies into doing anything that they don't want to do. However, we, their customers, keep them in business. If enough people begin requesting better food, a groundswell for healthier food will manifest. It takes two to play. Always remember this equation — they produce; we buy. That gives potential leverage.

It's the same with our restaurants. How much or little do our restaurants help our communities? We don't need to get self-righteous or nasty about it. The way to do it is to go to the restaurants that we patronize and say to them, "I want to help the environment and also want antibiotic free meat. I now that it's more expensive, and I don't want to pay more for it. But I would be willing to eat a smaller portion, perhaps four ounces of organic, antibiotic free chicken breast, instead of the six ounces of what is now served. Here's my name and telephone number. Call me when it's here. I love your restaurant."
And the same goes for shrimp. Tell them that Greg Christian taught you that sustainable shrimp costs forty-two percent more money, but that there's a great sustainable farm in Arizona called Desert Sweet Shrimp, and that if they will carry that, you would be willing to eat less shrimp for the same price. That is one way, and a very positive way, that we can move heaven and earth.

Looking back now, I am so grateful that I became an advocate and provider of organic food. It brings joy. One feels so fortunate to be able to advocate and serve food in so responsible a way. I was surrounded by young, bright people who came from all around the world, who shared in learning how to do this, people like Kim and Ritu and others. The biggest joy was that I was able to attract people who saw that they, too, could make money but also could make an enduring contribution to their community and environment. That is an entirely different kind of person, I have discovered. Not all were like that, but a majority were, and that was for me a pure joy. There were also pitfalls, including thinking that we were right and were done, and in every move we made, we discovered that there was more to do and further to go. I had to take care to remain as positive as I could, rather than abandoning myself to feeling helpless, since the prevailing food system and the entrenched thinking around it is both massive and constrictive. Another pitfall was a lack of humility. I struggle with that. Humility is key, and I remind myself each day that I am, at best, a mere vehicle through which the love and advancement may or may not manifest.

In retrospect, I realize that I sacrificed my catering company, an investment of more than seventeen years of labor and love, because I became so focused on so many projects, including educating farmers and speaking to anyone who would listen. I ended up taking my eye off the mother ship. I spent half my time with the Organic School Project and touring farms. I also made a couple of unwise hires and some bad decisions. Ironically, the thing that I was trying to move ended up being sacrificed in the process. It's not sad. I'm not mad. Other people took it much harder than I did. The rumors were flying in Chicago, most of them far-fetched and ridiculous. I regret having disappointed so many faithful customers when I had to close my business. Now looking back, in all honesty, I realize that I had some attachments that needed to be released. I was stuck in "I'm a caterer and a chef." I was also attached to being a successful business owner.

Having lost almost everything one has makes it easier to be open to whatever might be coming along life's new adventure. Perhaps I am meant to devote all of my time and energies to the Organic School Project and to helping people to raise their awareness about our current food system and how it could become vastly better and healthier. Let's face it: we've nearly killed our planet from the poisons we've put into it, in the air, the water, the soil, and our food. If we don't reverse this trend, humanity may not be around in a hundred years time.

Over six years ago, Chuck Skelton asked me why my food tasted so good, and I replied, "Because I love people." And he laughed and said, "Wow! I thought that was going to take longer." I do love people and I have come more and more to realize that truth and to open myself in love to others. It used to be that I could let down my guard with only my few trusted intimates; I now let it down all day long!

As I mentioned earlier, the forgiveness piece is something that I need to get better at. I find that it helps me to focus and stay on topic, especially with creative vision. It's harder and harder to throw me off the horse. It will be to no avail to recriminate the big companies; those who do so ultimately end up at a dead end and no one wins. If we can convince a lot of individuals to promote the accessibility of more local and organic food, in the name of helping the environment and our communities, perhaps the store owners will accommodate our requests and we will find ourselves healthier as well as living in a healthier world.

My daily practice of selfless service keeps me grounded and hopeful. I know that I am, at most, planting seeds, but I hope that those seeds will flourish once others recognize the value of the fruits that they offer. Part of my liberation to having been able to do what I have done happened when I made a fundamental choice not to sit around with like-minded people just talking the problem to death. That's easy. It doesn't really require very much, and it certainly doesn't do anything in a positive way. Supplying viable solutions to current problems is where I want to come from, just as I want to join with others who are willing and able to think outside the box.

108

When I now look back at my life, I comprehend all of my losses, gains, and failures in an entirely new context. Truly, it is that which I have lost that has taught me the most about myself, others and my profession, although I didn't recognize it at the time. Such adversities have allowed me to forge ahead, without worry about public impression, into visionary programs that challenge traditional expectation and thinking, wherein I have found tongues in the promise of a better future for our children and books in the willingness and eagerness of concerned individuals to make a positive difference. And the sermons from stones, as alluded to at the beginning of this memoir, are grounded in our need to forgive everyone, including ourselves, and to move ahead with courage and love, finding good in all things.

If this memoir has helped you, dear Reader, to see things in a new context, in a larger perhaps even more meaningful way, then I have fulfilled my purpose in writing it. If it impels to you positive action, then it has more than surpassed my hopes and expectations.

Chapter Eight
*The Organic School Project Today**

THE ORGANIC SCHOOL PROJECT is a dynamic and on-going program that constantly evolves and changes. For the most recent developments and offerings, please visit the project's web site:

http://www.organicschoolproject.org

The Organic School Project (OSP) provides school age children with a mindful foundation for a healthy and sustainable lifestyle through wellness programming initiatives.

OSP's primary program offering to combat youth health epidemics and build a sustainable future is the WELLNESS SERVICES MODEL. The Wellness Services Model is an education and food service systemic change approach to obesity prevention, comprised of three major components:

GROW, TEACH, FEED™

GROW: Organic, on-site community school gardens reconnect youth with their food sources while simultaneously providing experiential learning. OSP works with teachers to integrate the garden into existing curricula. Students are actively involved in every aspect of the gardens, from composting to planting to harvesting, so they can see first-hand where their food comes from and where it ends up.

TEACH: OSP educates youth on healthy lifestyles, mindfulness, and environmental stewardship through an integrated wellness curriculum, customized for schools in conjunction with faculty and students.

FEED: OSP feeds More Positive Foods™ through the school service system. OSP meals are made-from-scratch, organic and natural, and are sourced locally when seasonally available.

The Wellness Services Model was piloted at Alcott Elementary School in 2006-2007 and has been re-launched in the 2008-2009 school year.

For schools and school districts unable to implement the OSP Wellness Services Model, we offer OSP EXTENSION, a programming initiative aimed at providing a variety of wellness solutions for schools. These schools desire to work with OSP to provide youth with a strong foundation for sustainable lifestyles, enabling them to make positive choices fro themselves and the planet. OSP Extension can be customized for each school and can vary in duration and depth of programming.

*Note: All information shared in this chapter was taken directly from the Organic School Project web site. Please check with the current web site for updates and new programs and initiatives.

Chapter Nine
Bringing it Home, Making it Real

I HOPE THAT YOU'RE ASKING, "What can I do to help?"

Even the smallest of steps is important ... for such first steps can lead to ever increasing strides toward a healthier life style and a cleaner planet.

But before we explore ways to improve our current situation regarding food and its creation, let me simply ask you if you are aware of the following:

More than half the food we eat is bought from outside of America.

Almost all of the garlic we use comes from China.

The vast majority of food products for sale in Illinois have been procured from places that are thousands of miles away.

Over 95 percent of the organic foods being eaten in Illinois is not grown in Illinois.

Over 90 percent of the farmland in America grows five crops — corn, soy beans, rice, cotton and wheat.

Thirty-three million head of cattle are slaughtered every year — we eat an enormous amount of meat — most cattle are not allowed to walk around outside, but are instead consigned to feedlots.

Global food systems have crushed the local food systems in the United States, and the same is happening to countries around the world.

Natural flavors are mostly made in New Jersey — they are man made — as are most vitamins you read about on ingredient labels. These "natural" flavors are not well tested for potential long term effects. Scientists can make a drop of liquid chemical taste like anything, e.g. a greasy cheeseburger.

Therefore, when most people eat food, they think that they are eating what they appear to be eating because it looks and smells as it should — but in actuality, what they are eating is manufactured, made up, made to look and taste "real" although it is only chemicals.

People become addicted to these unnatural flavors and additives and they begin to crave them, and thus are prone to eating them again and again.

Over 6,000 chemicals are sanctioned for use in the processed-food industry, some with proven carcinogenic qualities. The human immune system correctly recognizes such food additives as toxic, and our immune systems go into overdrive to protect us. However, recurrent exposure to such chemicals gradually weakens the human immune system and an individual's ability to stave off disease.

Thus we live in a society that is becoming increasingly sick as people's immune systems are compromised by chemicals in food, water, cleaning supplies, clothes, carpets, bed sheets, and so on.

In effect, our food industry shook hands with the devil years ago when it decided to trade quality of taste and freshness for longevity of shelf-life, the better to keep products viable for sale for longer intervals. As I mentioned earlier in this memoir, many older people can still remember when food tasted better, and there are many good reasons why it did. In the name of increased profits, the food industry opted for the extensive use of fertilizers for larger yields, additives for longer shelf life, and widespread mechanization for lower costs. Our food today rarely passes through human hands, unless it is organic.

Where can we begin to make a difference? I would suggest that it can start with small things, such as caring enough and taking time to read labels. A good rule to follow is if you can't pronounce the ingredients in a food product, you may be better off not buying it. In fact, I would recommend that investigating the most common ingredients of our food stuffs would be a good first step. How many of us know what high fructose corn syrup is, or soy lecithin? Most of us are not trained chemists. Begin doing that kind of personal research, raise your consciousness, and then make an informed choice.

It is important to know where our food comes from as well as how it is produced. One of my neighbors grills a lot of chicken breast each week, because that is one of the staples of her chosen diet. I would invite her to engage in some in-depth research of her preferred brand and then to investigate that company's website and ultimately to e-mail their information officer with whatever questions she might have related to that product and its health record. Once you get into the habit of doing that with one area of inquiry, it sort of spills over into other areas.

I hope people will return to cooking their meals from scratch, so that they will reconnect with Mother Earth. Most of us in this society are disconnected right now, and in losing that connection we also lose that deeper sense of who we really are and what we can do. We become, in fact, alienated from ourselves — strangers, if you will. Look around. People don't focus on the good they do; instead, they emphasize the negative. They have lost respect both for themselves and others. What if those same people decided to go organic and to begin, in a small way, a network through which they could buy and enjoy organic foods? What if they went to visit a local organic farmer every month and got his story? And then went back each month to learn more about him and his family and what he does and why he does it?

Respect can only come from the sincere expression of gratitude, humility, and compassion. If we could perhaps take a first step and always be mindful and grateful for our daily food and daily bread, and be prayerfully grateful throughout the day, what a wonderful first step that would be. Something so basic and beautiful would be an entry point that might prove to be transforming. If we could only begin to look at the preparation and eating of food as a sacrament and an affirmation of life, how would that change this world? But it is hard to stay in that frame of mindset in this hurly-burly, rush-rush world; our obligations and responsibilities intrude and cause us to tumble back to hard reality. However, if we, on a daily basis, made it our intention to create a new reality where we would honor everything and everyone and would be mindful of our food and grateful for its presence and sustenance, perhaps that harsh reality would not keep tumbling back.

Recently I needed to get my CD player fixed, but the first advice I received was to merely buy a new, since they are so inexpensive. Then I began to envision what would happen to my CD player. I didn't want it to go the dump. We have tons of old electronic equipment (computers, televisions, CD players, and so on) and don't know how to dispose of it safely, and just shipping that junk to the Third World doesn't really solve the problem.

Too often we allow ourselves into being fooled into thinking that we need to buy something that we neither need nor want. We are continually bombarded by commercials via newspapers, radio, and television. The commercials trick us into thinking that we really have a choice in what we buy, but in truth they take away our autonomy. They create an ever increasing disconnect between us and nature, and we lose touch with the real world . Commercials, when we fall prey to their spells, turn us into purchasers, perhaps better described as consumers, and we rush out to buy stuff we don't really need and probably don't really want. We may think we want it for a while, but how long does that afterglow of desire last? We live in a society where we become programmed consumers.

That advertising is effective there can be no question. Else wise, why would there still be so much of it if it didn't work, and work well? I remember hearing recently that half of the cost of an automobile, or something akin to that percentage, is for the advertising that it takes to sell the vehicle. That's crazy. And I'm sure that this percentage is not restricted solely to the automobile industry.

In the average mainline grocery store, there are over 45,000 items that can be chosen. However, since we are well programed to choose certain products, it might be more accurate to say that the products have us rather than that we have them. When I was drinking, the beer at the store *had me*, if you know what I mean, even though at that time *I thought I had the beer*. However, one can distant one's self from these

115

subtle and hidden pressures, and one of the best ways of doing it is to avoid television and other media where advertising is rampant. For example, I happen to like cookies. Sometimes I choose to eat them around a holiday, knowing that they may not be the best thing for me, but it is important to remember that *I am choosing them.* They don't have me.

I have been given the gift of *knowing* what people need, even if I have never met them before. The intuition happens of its own accord and surrounds the creating process wherein people who are eating the food I have prepared will exclaim, "I feel better! That is *so* good." They say those things because their hearts have been opened, and it's not anything that "I" have done, but rather something that was allowed to flow through me, because I was able to get out of the way of my own ego, and simply surrender myself to wanting to serve that gift. I can't emphasize enough how important it is that any sense of "I" is excluded from this miraculous and wonderful process. Perhaps it's no more than allowing one's self to "flow with God." When this exchange happens, the person who marvels at the food and feels better has experienced a larger opening of heart and soul. Perhaps that person's consciousness has even been raised. I am reminded of the 1987 Academy Award winning Danish film *Babette's Feast*, based on a story by Isak Dinesen, that so clearly showed how wonderfully redeeming and transforming food can be when it is prepared with love and in the name of love.

In truth, it has everything to do with the combination of foods and nothing to do with the combination of foods. All of great chefs are combining ingredients all the time, but it's not in the recipe. The secret lies in the "flow" — and the magic never happens if those cooking think even for a millisecond that they are better than the fire, smarter than the cow. It is the humility that matters — that can bring lasting results by opening the door to a much larger perfection and incarnation that literally descends through the maker and brings transformation.

In many kitchens, when a chef overcooks something, say a piece of salmon, he will toss it and simply get a new piece. However, I tell anyone under my care that when they overcook something, they need to remember the larger context of what they have done. It took salmon a year to become a salmon and it took maybe twenty guys with twenty-five years of experience to catch it, and maybe 150 guys who made the boat, and their wives the clothing and feeding their kids, and then the guy who takes the salmon to market and the people who made the nets, and those who transport it — so, finally, we have a million years of collective effort in one six ounce piece of salmon — so, how dare anyone overcook something so precious? And everyone gets it.

When you respect all of the above, both in its simple beauty and utter complexity, that is the vehicle through which there is a chance to become humble and a vehicle through which prepared food can be transforming for those who eat it. If one is humble and remains mindful, the opportunity of preparing and serving something to someone else in love is much more of a potentiality than not.

We are talking about the sacred and that which makes life worth living. We are talking about surrendering to the present moment.

If we keep surrendering, finally there is nothing left but God.

My hope is that all who read this memoir will find that their hearts have opened to the wonderful possibilities that await our claiming them, that those readers will look in the mirror to see and to acknowledge their unique gifts, and then move to loving action wherein those gifts will in turn help others on the journey.

~Parting Thoughts~
Please Consider . . .

In all that you have thus far read, I hope that you are contemplating the suggestion that one of the highest leverage points in moving our planet toward sustainability — toward respecting Mother Earth, Nature, and the resources of all the peoples on our planet — is through our food system.

If you can eat more local and organic foods, please consider increasing those in your diet, for that is a very good thing to do, both for your personal health and for the planet.

If you can eat less meat and fish, that's also a help. If you do eat meat and fish, be sure to eat that which has been treated with dignity. It's even better if you can take the step to know of the farmer who raised the food or meat or who runs the fish farm. The more personal you can be with the people who bring you your food, the better it is for you.

The more respected the farmer, the farm, the animals, the fish, the crop — the better it is for you and your family.

Knowing where your food that you buy comes from on the front end is much more important than recycling and/or composting, although those are also really important to do. People are busy cutting out using little bottles of water, not realizing that a pound of beef goes through at least 2,400 gallons of water to come to market.

The first question of general **consumption** is: Do you really need it? The second question is: Can I find this item used or somewhere not new? If it's food related, the third **question** is: Can I find it made or grown locally?

People should forget about changing whatever they are trying to change. People also need to own their part for where we are today, whether it's big or small, regarding our draining of Mother Earth's resources and filling up dumps with garbage. We need to forgive ourselves and also others — we have all contributed to creating the current situation in which we find ourselves. And, finally, we need to vote with our dollars and move our families and business in that way, for the sake of a healthier community and better world.

With grateful thanks . . .

The following are people, foundations and corporations that have supported Organic School Project. There are many more people to thank that helped pave the path of Organic School Project=s journey. Thank you to all of those, mentioned and unmentioned, who have given their time, money, energy and support to help build this organization.

Board of Directors, past and present

_ Rakesh Amin
_ Dr. Tom Duffy
_ Dr. Martha Grout
_ Peter Grumhaus
_ Heather Hilleren
_ Stacey Lawson
_ Tom McGarrity
_ John Rudy
_ Bob Scaman
_ Kim Silver
_ Jeff Shane
_ Diana Smith

Chicago Public Schools & Chartwells-Thompson

_ Bob Bloomer
_ Carmen Crespo
_ Dave Domovic
_ Louise Esaian
_ Janet House
_ Marvis Jackson-Ivy
_ Jennifer Malchow
_ Susie Novak

- Elaine Reitz
- Rinku Patel
- Linda Salinas
- Sue Susanke
- Hector Quintana

Partners, Advocates & Supporters
- Will & Erika Allen
- Phil Aucutt
- Patsy Benveniste
- Mayor Richard Daley
- Rochelle Davis
- Chuck Dumont
- Ken Dunn
- Elisa Durso Fischer
- Monica Eng
- Reven & Reed Fellars
- Deepa Handu
- Tali Hylen
- Sadhu Johnston
- Joanne Kouba
- John Koubek
- Mark & Martha Morgan Laubacher
- Robin Lavin
- Kafryn Lieder
- Leslie Manzara
- Katie McDougall
- Paul & Michal Miller
- Lindsay Norwood
- Carla Nuzzo
- Gerry Podraza
- Cynthia ???
- Rachel Ray
- Mark Reed & Nora Herbst

- Kathleen Rude & John Mullin
- Sara Snow
- Gordon Sinclair
- Ilyse Strongin-Bombicino
- Mrs. Walsh
- Alice Waters
- Kerry & Sarah Wood

Staff, past and present
- Tessa Bergan
- Carrie Cruz
- Maureen George
- Sen Haines
- Cheri Helmick
- Kim Guster
- Sarah Krull
- Diana Lauber
- Stephanie Szuts
- Meg Trausch
- Carina Vallejos
- Josephine Lauer Washuk

Foundations & Corporations
- A Cooler Planet
- Annie=s Natural Foods Inc.
- Brico Fund, LLC
- ChapterOne Organics
- Chicago Community Trust
- Chipotle
- CLOCC
- Delmonte ADo Something@
- DOC=s Juice and Smoothies
- Drew=s Eatery
- The Field Foundation

- Freddie Mac Foundation Matching Gift
- Laroux Creek Food Corporation
- LaSalle Bank
- Lazzara Family Foundation
- The Little Owl Foundation (Donor Advised Fund of The Chicago Community Trust)
- Lumpkin Family Foundation
- New Frontiers Foundation
- Newman=s Own Foundation
- Northern Trust Charitable Giving Program
- Organic Valley Midwest
- Osa Foundation
- Polk Bros. Foundation
- Walsh Foundation
- Whole Foods Foundation

References for further reading

Ableman M. *From the Good Earth: A Celebration of Growing Food Around the World*. New York: Abrams; 1993.

Ableman M. *On Good Land: An Autobiography of an Urban Farm*. San Francisco: Chronicle Books; 1998.

Ard JD, Rosati R, Oddone EZ. Culturally-sensitive weight loss program produces significant reduction in weight, blood pressure and cholesterol in eight weeks. *JAMA*. 2001;92:515-523.

Ard JD, Carter-Edwards L, Svetkey, LP. A new model for developing and executing culturally appropriate behavior modification clinical trials for African Americans. *Ethn Dis*. 2003;13:279-285.

Babu SC, Nivas BT, Traxler GJ. Irrigation development and environmental degradation in developing countries--a dynamic model of investment decisions and policy options. *Water Resource Manag*. 1996; 10:129-146.

Belasco W, Scranton P, eds. *Food Nations: Selling Taste in Consumer Societies*. New York: Routledge; 2002.

Counihan C, Van Esterik P, eds. *Food and Culture: A Reader*. London: Routledge; 1997.

Bohm RA, Essenburg TJ, Fox WF. Sustainability of potable water services in the Philippines. *Water Resour Res*. 1993;29:1955-1963.

Brownell KD, Warner K. The perils of ignoring history: Big Tobacco played dirty and millions died; How similar is Big Food? Paper submitted for publication.

Brownell KD, Horgen KB. *Food Fight: The Inside Story of the Food Industry, America's Obesity Crisis, and What We Can Do About It.* New York: McGraw-Hill/Contemporary Books; 2004.

Brownell KD, Horgen KB. *Food Fight: The Inside Story of the Food Industry, America's Obesity Crisis, and What We Can Do About It.* New York: McGraw Hill/Contemporary Books; 2004.

Campbell A J Self-regulation and the media. *Federal Communications Law Journal.* 1999; 51: 711.

Center for Science in the Public Interest. Pestering Parents. *How food companies market obesity to children.* Available at: www.cspinet.org/pesteringparents.

Chou S-Y, Grossman M, Safer H. An economic analysis of adult obesity: results from the Behavioral Risk Factor Surveillance System. *J Health Econ.* 2004; 23: 565-87.

Critser G. (2003). *Fat Land: How Americans Became the Fattest People in the World.* Boston: Houghton Mifflin.

Gardner BL. *American Agriculture in the Twentieth Century: How It Flourished and What It Cost.* Cambridge, MA: Harvard University Press; 2002.

Becker E. Trade group to cut farm subsidies for rich nations. *New York Times*. 2004 Aug

Drewnowski A, Barratt-Fornell A. Do healthier diets cost more? *Nutr Today*. 2004;29:161-8.

Donation S. *Madison & Vine: Why the Entertainment & Advertising Industries Must Converge to Survive.* New York: McGraw Hill; 2004.

Kessler DA. *A Question of Intent: A Great American Battle with a Deadly Industry.* New York: Public Affairs, 2002.

Schwartz MB, Brownell KD. Future directions for preventive action on obesity. In: Crawford D, Jeffrey R, editors. *Obesity prevention in the 21st century: Public health approaches to tackle the obesity pandemic.* Oxford: Oxford University Press; 2005.

Printed in the United States
148900LV00001B/1/P

9 780982 470602